SEEK AND
EXPECT
MIRACLES

Glenn Rawson

ISBN 979-888526327-6

Printed in the United States of America

10 9 8 7 6 5 4 3 2

FREE WEEKLY STORIES DELIVERED TO YOUR INBOX

SUBSCRIBE AT
GLENNRAWSONSTORIES.COM

THANKS TO THE GLENN RAWSON STORIES TEAM:

DIANNA, JASON, JEAN, KRISTEN, AND SARA FOR THEIR
TALENTS AND EFFORT TO HELP MAKE THIS BOOK POSSIBLE.

Other Inspirational Titles By Glenn

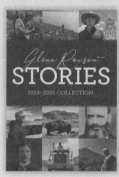
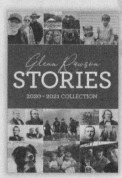

Get These Great Titles At
GlennRawsonStories.com

Customer Submitted Book Reviews

"Thank you for all your time spent researching all these stories and then sharing them each Sunday!"

- Luna Canfield

"I just got my book and I am amazed with it. I can't stop reading it. I was not dissapointed at all. Great book to own."

- Lisa Denise Kerr

"I ordered two. One for myself and the other for a favorite cousin. We both love the books. They arrived quickly and are wonderful reads!"

- Shutterbug Carol

Subscribe to Glenn's Stories at
GlennRawsonStories.com

"In the same way, the Lord will bless you with miracles if you believe in Him," he said.
"Do the spiritual work to seek miracles."

-Russell M. Nelson, The Power of Spiritual Momentum

TABLE OF CONTENTS

Table Of Contents

x

PROLOGUE

The ministering of angels is a sign to all the world of God's people. It has always been—since the days of Adam—down to the present time. When angels minister among a people, there God and His gospel are also. Moreover, the ministering of angels is one of the gifts of the Spirit, given unto men to bless their fellows.

Therefore, it should be no surprise that members of The Church of Jesus Christ of Latter-day Saints have a rich history and experience with ministering angels. Those angels have come to young and old, male and female alike, with messages of comfort and guidance from the Almighty.

This book is a glimpse and a touch of some of that history. It is a glance back at a small handful of those experiences that have been deemed appropriate to share. The purpose of this book is to edify and inspire faith. Indeed, even as President Russell M. Nelson invited the April 2022 General Conference, we should "seek and expect miracles."

Glenn Rawson

Can You Help Us

In 1982, Sister Margaret E. Poole O'Brien was serving as a proselyting senior sister missionary in the Henderson Nevada Mission for The Church of Jesus Christ of Latter-day Saints. One day, she and her companion came home for lunch and a midday rest. Sister O'Brien was in her room studying, when she heard a quiet voice say, "The Lucier family needs food." Sister O'Brien said:

> "I didn't pay much attention to it and went on with my studying, thinking this can't be right. This family lived in a lovely home and seemed to be quite well off. But shortly, the voice came again with the exact same message: 'the Lucier family needs food.'

> This time, I listened and made the comment, 'I would see what I could do.' I went out to our little kitchen, just as [my companion], Sister Hess, came out from her bedroom. She went right over to the fridge and looked inside. I asked her what she was doing, and she said, 'I had the impression that the Lucier family needs food.' I then told her what I had heard and she said the message had come to her in a dream, but it was so real.

> We took what we thought they might use out of our fridge. This filled two big grocery sacks and it pretty well cleaned out the refrigerator. We then took what money we had, went to Albertson's grocery store, and bought everything we thought they might like–even a big watermelon. We spent all of the money we had. We loaded the food into the car and began to drive to Lucier's home, when Sister

Hess pulled over and stopped the car. She said, 'What if we got the wrong impression? What if they don't need this food? What shall we do then?' After a prayer, we decided to go on to their place, but before we would take the food in, we would go to the door empty-handed, just to check on things."

That is what they did. Lucier's nine-year-old son answered the door and seemed especially excited to see them. He called to the rest of the family, "The missionaries are here. The missionaries are here." Sister O'Brien continued:

"As we walked in, we could see that their table was set nicely for dinner. The mother kept saying, 'We knew you would come. We have been praying to the Lord for your help.' We asked her how we could help. Crying, she said, as she led us into the dining room, 'I have cooked this potato and cut it into 5 pieces for our dinner. This is the last of our food.'

She then went on to explain that they had made an unwise investment that had taken all their money, and on the very day they received this terrible news, Brother Lucier had lost his job. "We don't know what to do," Sister Lucier said, "Can you help us?"

The sisters invited them to come out to the car. Sister O'Brien said, "They couldn't believe it when they saw all the groceries. They were so happy. They kept asking us, 'How did you know to bring us food? How did you know we needed you?' Of course, we told them that our Heavenly Father had answered their prayers and He had told us that they were in need."

The story would be evidence enough of the "multitude of the Lord's tender mercies" if it ended right there, but it does not. The two missionaries had barely gotten home when their phone rang. A friend who worked part-time at

Albertsons told them that his boss had given him sacks and sacks of food that the store was getting rid of and he wanted to share with them. Sister O'Brien concluded:

> "We drove right over to his place and he and his wife loaded our car with sacks full of food. We thanked them with tears in our eyes, drove back home, and began to carry everything into the house. As we put things away in the refrigerator, we could see it was much more than we had taken out of our fridge to take to the Lucier family. With our refrigerator completely full and our hearts full of wonder and gratitude, we knelt to thank our Heavenly Father."

Source:

Kareen M. Springer, Highland, Utah (daughter of Sister O'Brien)

He Will Meet You at the Sweetwater

Robert and Seviah Cunningham Egbert were married on April 1, 1846. Shortly after, they left to follow Brigham Young and the twelve apostles to the west. It was while they were on the Missouri River that Captain James Allen of the United States Army came asking for volunteers to join the war with Mexico. At President Young's urging, Robert volunteered and was assigned to Company A. He left his new bride, Seviah, at Winter Quarters and marched away to California on July 20, 1846.

Seviah was there on the Missouri River in that terrible winter of 1846-47, when so many of the saints suffered and died. She heard nothing from Robert the entire time he was gone.

The Battalion was discharged in July 1847, in Los Angeles, and the men scattered and began to make their way back to their families. However, when Robert did not return by the spring of 1848, Seviah decided to go west. With help from Robert's brother, she got outfitted and started across the plains.

As she journeyed, Seviah became very worried about Robert. Other Battalion men had returned—but where was he? Was he alive or dead? The following account comes from the family records:

> "Traveling along the dusty road, she was so lonely and wished so much to know where her husband was and if she would ever see him again. She became so wrought up over his absence that she cried as she drove along. All at once, she looked up

and saw a man coming from the opposite direction. Very strange, she thought, as there were no humans except Indians for hundreds of miles. She tried, as he drew near, to hide her face in her bonnet. The road was narrow and he could hardly turn out past the wagon for the high brush on both sides of the road. When he turned out enough to get out of the way of the horses, he stopped by her wagon and inquired if she was Robert's wife. She said, 'Yes.' She supposed it was a messenger from California, who had seen her husband. He said, 'Here is a letter from your husband to you.' She took it and saw it was written in his own handwriting. It said he was well and would meet her at the head of Sweetwater. She looked up to thank him, but he was nowhere in sight. When they came to a place where they could get by, her brother-in-law, Joseph, stepped up to the wagon and asked her who the man was and what he wanted. She told him about the letter and went to get it to show him, but the letter was gone and she could not find it. She rejoiced and her spirits were buoyed up and she did not cry any more."

Seviah's company finally arrived at the Sweetwater. As they rolled into the camping area, there were people already there. She looked hard to see if she could see Robert. Imagine her surprise when Robert walked up to her wagon and found her first.

Robert had spent the winter of 47-48 in Salt Lake and then turned east in the spring to find his family. He had expected to travel all the way to Council Bluffs, but as the emigrants rolled into his camp that night on the Sweetwater, he happened to see a team and outfit that looked strangely like his own. When he walked over to investigate, he found his dear wife, Seviah. We can only imagine the joy of their reunion. Seviah explained:

> "I told him about the letter I had received. He said he had never written a letter as he had no way of sending one to her. They both marveled over this strange experience and declared it was one of the three Nephites who had written and gave her the letter, and the strange thing was, he actually did meet her [at the Sweetwater]. They arrived in Salt Lake Valley in the fall of 1848."

Source:

https://www.familysearch.org/tree/person/memories/KN34-9S3

3
Chapter Three
Here Is Little Margaret

On September 2, 1847, on the Sweetwater River in Wyoming, Margaret Grant, the infant daughter of Jedediah and Caroline Grant, succumbed to cholera. She was buried on the side of a rolling, clay hill, not far from the trail. Her mother "[wept] as if her heart would break." Yet, notwithstanding the grief, the wagon train hitched up and moved on.

With the loss of her baby, Caroline Grant grew weaker and weaker. Then Sunday, September 26, 1847, somewhere south of present-day Evanston ,Wyoming, Caroline was critically ill. For the first time, there was no Sabbath singing or preaching heard in the camp. Instead, the day was passed in fasting and prayer for Caroline's recovery. Around midnight, Caroline closed her eyes and seemed to be sinking. To her husband, Jedediah, she whispered, "All is well! All is well! Please take me to the Valley—Jeddy. Get Margaret—bring her to me!"

"Brother Grant answered tenderly…as he sobbed with sorrow, 'Yes, yes, Caroline. I'll do my best. I'll do my best.'"

The next morning, Jedediah Grant, true to his promise, set out for Salt Lake City with his beloved Caroline. Two days later, he would lay her to rest in the Valley. The entire community grieved at his loss. Caroline Grant was only 29 years-old, and the first white woman buried in the Salt Lake Valley.

Days later, Jedediah and a friend, Joseph Bates Noble, sat close to a small fire under the night sky of Wyoming. Jedediah requested that they sing some hymns. When they finished, Jedediah "sat with bowed head for some time, then he looked up, glowing with his former inspiration... and declared in a firm voice...'Bates, God has made it plain. The joy of paradise where my wife and baby are together, seems to be upon me tonight. For some wise purpose, they have been released from the earth struggles into which you and I are plunged. They are many, many times happier than we can possibly be here.'"

Days later, Jedediah and Bates reached the place where Margaret was buried. Noble described the events:

> "A few paces from the little grave, we stopped hesitatingly...and stood with eyes fixed before us. Neither tried to speak. An ugly hole replaced the small mound; and so recently had the wolves departed that every sign was fresh before us. I dared not raise my eyes to look at Jedediah. From the way I felt, I could but guess his feelings. Like statues of the wilderness, we stood grown to the spot, each fully realizing that nothing more could be done. After several minutes of silent tears, we quietly withdrew, carrying away again only that which we had brought."

Now moving forward nine years to November 1856— Jedediah Grant, now grievously ill himself, was granted a vision. He saw the world of spirits into which all will one day enter. He described the paradise of God as a heavenly place; beautiful beyond all description, filled with gardens, flowers, and buildings more glorious than anything found in this sphere. It was a place of perfect order, light, and cleanliness—a place of peace. Caroline came to him speaking words of comfort and instruction. She was beautiful. Margaret, too, was there, both glorious witnesses that the terrible tragedy of the plains was and would be overcome in the Paradise of God. On the night of December 1, 1856, Jedediah M. Grant passed into the world of spirits.

Source:

https://www.churchofjesuschrist.org/manual/church-history-in-the-fulness-of-times/chapter-twenty-seven?lang=eng

4
Chapter Four
I Have Come to Watch Over You

The following experience of President Wilford Woodruff illustrates that angels watch over us and are concerned about how we live. It is vital to their interest that we live so as to be able to carry on the work they started.

"I believe the eyes of the heavenly hosts are over this people; I believe they are watching the elders of Israel, the prophets and apostles and men who are called to bear off this kingdom. I believe they watch over us all with great interest.

I will here make a remark concerning my own feelings. After the death of Joseph Smith, I saw and conversed with him many times in my dreams in the night season. On one occasion, he and his brother Hyrum met me when on the sea going on a mission to England. I had Dan Jones with me. He received his mission from Joseph Smith before his death; and the prophet talked freely to me about the mission I was then going to perform. He also talked to me with regard to the mission of the Twelve Apostles in the flesh, and he laid before me the work they had to perform; and he also spoke of the reward they would receive after death. There were many other things he laid before me in his interview on that occasion. When I awoke, many of the things he had told me were taken from me, and I could not comprehend them.

I have had many interviews with Brother Joseph until the last 15 or 20 years of my life; I have not seen him for that length of time. But during my travels in the southern country last winter, I had many interviews with President Young, and with Heber C. Kimball, and Geo. A. Smith, and Jedediah M. Grant, and many others who are dead. They attended our conference. They attended our meetings.

On one occasion, I saw Brother Brigham and Brother Heber ride in a carriage ahead of the carriage in which I rode when I was on my way to attend a conference; and they were dressed in the most priestly robes. When we arrived at our destination, I asked President Young if he would preach to us. He said, "No, I have finished my testimony in the flesh. I shall not talk to this people any more. But (said he) I have come to see you; I have come to watch over you, and to see what the people are doing. Then (said he) I want you to teach the people—and I want you to follow this counsel yourself—that they must labor and so live as to obtain the Holy Spirit, for without this you cannot build up the kingdom. Without the Spirit of God, you are in danger of walking in the dark, and in danger of failing to accomplish your calling as apostles and as elders in the church and kingdom of God. And, said he, Brother Joseph taught me this principle. "And I will here say, I have heard him refer to that while he was living. But what I was going to say is this: the thought came to me that Brother Joseph had left the work of watching over this church and kingdom to others, and that he had gone ahead, and that he had left this work to men who have lived and labored with us since he left us. This idea manifested itself to me, that such men advance in the Spirit World. And I believe myself that these men who have died and gone into the Spirit World had this mission left with them, that is, a certain portion of them, to watch over the Latter-day Saints." (Journal of Discourses, 21:318)

President Woodruff later referred to the same experience in a stake conference of the Weber Stake. He said:

> "Every man and woman in this Church should labor to get that Spirit. We are surrounded by these evil spirits that are at war against God and against everything looking to the building up of the kingdom of God; and we need this Holy Spirit to enable us to overcome these influences."

Source:

Deseret Weekly, 7 Nov. 1896, p. 643. As cited in Howard W. Hunter, "Developing Spirituality," Ensign, May 1979, 24.

I Heard a Plain Voice

In 1847-1848, the Samuel and Elvira Steele family was living in Mt. Pisgah, Iowa. They were a part of the great exodus of the Latter-day Saints from Nauvoo to the Rocky Mountains.

According to family history, Samuel left his wife and family for a time and went to work about 200 miles away. Many of the Saints at that time traveled south and found work in northern Missouri. It is presumed that Samuel did the same. While he was gone, his three-year-old daughter, Lovina, was playing before the fire, when a hot coal popped onto her dress and set it ablaze. In panic, Lovina ran outside, where the wind caught the fire and spread it. A neighbor saw Lovina and ran to help. The fire was extinguished, but Lovina was badly burned. The family joined together in fasting and prayer for Lovina's recovery and that her father Samuel would come home.

Meanwhile, Samuel and a friend had completed the long winter journey and had indeed found the work that was promised. One night, as they left a prayer meeting, Samuel announced to his friend that he, "must start home in the morning." His partner was surprised. "We have just got located and ready to work," he said. Brother Steele said, "While the meeting was going on, I heard a plain voice saying you are wanted at home. One of your family is ill and nigh unto death." Brother Steele was determined to go, but his partner said, "It is winter, the snow is deep, the weather is cold, no

conveyance, no road broke." Brother Steele said he must go home.

Samuel traveled two day's journey toward home, when he met friends who were on their way to Pisgah with a horse and sleigh. They offered Samuel a ride. Upon arriving home, he learned that his daughter had been severely burned and was very low and near death. He later described in graphic detail just how severe her wounds were. The family was surprised to see him. He explained the voice he heard and the message. Curious, they questioned him as to the exact time the message was received. They then told him, "That night, that hour, that minute, we were all in a fast meeting, praying to the Lord to send you home."

Lovina would recover, but carry those scars the rest of her life. She came on to the Salt Lake Valley, married Benjamin Franklin Barrus, and settled in Grantsville. This was not the only moment when this hardy pioneer woman proved the steel of her faith.

Source:

https://www.familysearch.org/tree/person/memories/KWN2-841

6
Chapter Six

I Must Freeze and Die

It was January 1856, in Salt Lake City, Utah. Twenty-three-year-old Marriner Wood Merrill was hauling logs out of North Mill Creek Canyon. The logs were used to make houses. It was a cold winter, and the temperature at times -20-30 degrees Fahrenheit. On one of those very cold days, Marriner was in the canyon alone. He had cut the five logs he needed and had them placed side by side, in preparation for loading on his bobsleigh. He got the first log on the sleigh and turned to load the others. He described what happened next:

"The one I had on the sled slipped off like it was shot out of a gun and struck me in the hollow of the legs and threw me forward on my face across the four logs lying on the ground, or ice. In falling, my hand spike, which I had used in loading the first log, slipped out of my hand and out of my reach. And thus, I found myself with my body lying face downwards across the four logs and the fifth log lying across my legs. I was pinned to the ground with a heavy red pine log, 10 inches through at the large end and 22 feet long, lying across my legs. There I was with no visible means to extricate myself and there was no aid at hand, as no one but myself was in the canyon that day.

I made up my mind that I must freeze and die all alone in the mountains of Utah. Many serious thoughts passed through my mind, as you may imagine. In falling on the logs, my breast and stomach were hurt and it was difficult for me to breathe. I did not conceive what to do under the trying ordeal, but concluded to ask the Lord to help me, which I did in earnest prayer. After calling upon the Lord for some time, I began to make an effort to extricate myself, but all in vain, as I could not move the log that was lying on me. I, however, continued my efforts until I was exhausted and lost all recollection of my situation.

The first I remembered [afterward], I was one mile down the canyon, sitting on my load of logs and the oxen going gently along. My overcoat was by the side of me, and I was feeling very cold…. I looked at the load and found I had the five logs on the sled, three on the bottom and two on the top, nicely bound, my ax sticking in the top log, my whip lying on the load by my side, my sheepskin (with the wool on, which I used to sit on) also on the load, and I sitting on it. I made an effort to get off the load and put on my overcoat, but found I could not do it, as I was so sore in my legs and breast that it was with great difficulty that I could move at all. …I was confined to the house for some days before I could get around again. Who it was that extricated me from under the log, loaded my sled, hitched my oxen to it, and placed me on it, I cannot say, as I do not now, or even then at the time, remember seeing anyone, and I know for a surety no one was in the canyon that day but myself. Hence, I must give the Lord, or my guardian angel, credit for saving my life in extricating me from such a perilous situation."

Source:

Utah Pioneer and Apostle Marriner Wood Merrill and His Family, edited by Melvin Clarence Merrill, 1937, pages 44-45

 16

I Saw a Halo of Light

Samuel Taylor Orton was a handcart pioneer who joined the Church in England and came to Zion as part of the Edward Bunker Handcart Company in 1856. This experience occurred while he was on that journey.

"We got along very well until we got within two or three hundred miles of Utah, when our provisions began to get very low or about ¼ pound of flour per day. Being a young man of about 24 years of age, I soon became very weak and sick, so I had to leave my handcart and travel behind the company.

I was so sick I thought I should die, and I asked the Lord that I might die. All at once, a voice spoke to me as plain as I ever heard a voice in my life and said, "Sam, are you here?" I turned around and answered 'Yes,' but could see no one, which surprised me very much.

I went on and caught up with the company, took hold of my handcart, and my sickness left me. This set me to thinking. What do you expect to see when you get to Salt Lake City? I made up my mind if the Father and the Son did appear to the Prophet Joseph Smith and reveal the gospel unto him, and that Brigham Young was his lawful successor, I wanted to see the halo of light around his head like there was around the head of the Savior on nearly all of the pictures we see.

All this passed from my mind until we reached Salt Lake City on the 5th of October. The next morning,

I went to a meeting in the Old Bowery, and took my seat about the middle of the building. The people were coming in pretty lively. I was watching to see if there was any one I knew, but saw no one. Looking toward the stand, there I saw President Young, with the rays of light around his head as I had asked for on the plains, and the same voice as spoke to me on the plains said,

'Now Sam, if ever you apostatize, here is your condemnation.'

I looked around me to see if the people heard it, but I thought they did not.

Source:

https://history.lds.org/overlandtravels/sources/2942/orton-samuel-taylor-record-book-ca-1877-1904-fd-1-35-36

https://ancestors.familysearch.org/en/KW8D-DVY/samuel-taylor-orton-1832-1907

I Saw Three Strangers

Marie Madaline Cardon was born on July 6, 1834, at St Bartholomew, Italy. She was a descendant of the Vaudois or Waldensians; a mountain people who had existed and suffered for centuries high up in the Alps, for the sake of their religion. When Marie was about six years old, she received a very remarkable manifestation which would change not only her life, but also that of her family for generations. These are her words:

"I was upstairs in bed. A strange feeling came over me. It appeared that I was a young woman instead of a mere child. I thought I was on a small strip of meadow, close to our vineyard, keeping my father's milk cows from the vineyard. It seemed that I was sitting on the grass reading a Sunday School book. I looked up and saw three strangers in front of me. As I looked into their faces, I dropped my eyes instantly, being very much frightened. Suddenly, the thought came to me that I must look at them so that I might remember them in the future. I raised my eyes and looked them straight in the face. One of them, seeing that I was afraid, said: 'Fear not, for we are the servants of God and have come from afar to preach unto the world the everlasting Gospel, which has been restored to the earth in these last days, for the redemption of mankind.'

They told me that God had spoken from the heavens and had revealed His everlasting Gospel to the young boy, Joseph Smith, that it should never more be taken away again; that His kingdom would be set up and that all the honest in heart would be gathered together. They told me that I would be the means of bringing my parents and family into this great gathering. Moreover, the day was not far off when we would leave our homes and cross the great ocean. We would travel across the wilderness and go to Zion, where we could serve God according to the dictates of our conscience. When they had finished their message to me, they said they would return soon and visit us. They took some small books from their pockets and gave them to me, saying: 'Read these and learn'. They then disappeared, instantly."

Marie shared the dream with her family, who believed her. Then, in 1850, word reached the family of three Latter-day Saint elders preaching in a neighboring town. Greatly excited, her father dressed in his Sunday best and went to find them. He listened to them preach and then asked them to come home with him. On the way, he told them of Marie's dream. When they entered the house, Marie was not there. She said:

"When the elders reached our home that Sunday evening, they inquired for me, being interested in what my father had told them concerning me. I was not at the house at the time, but I was out on a small strip of meadow land. It seemed to be the identical spot I had seen in that vision of childhood so many years before. I was sitting on the grass reading a Sunday School book. I did not hear them until my father said to the elders, 'This is my daughter who had the vision or dream concerning the strangers, who told me to fear not, for they were the servants of God.' Upon being introduced, I shook hands with each of them. They took some tracts or small books from their pockets and spoke the very same words I heard in the dream or vision."

Not long after, Marie and the members of her family were baptized, notwithstanding the fierce opposition and persecution by mobbers and ministers. One Sabbath, as they gathered for worship, a mob surrounded the house "yelling and shrieking most hideously." They demanded the elders and the girl who was helping them be turned over. Marie, with Bible in hand, walked out and faced the mob. She relates:

> "It became evident that they were on the verge of pouncing upon the elders. I raised my right hand in which I held my Bible and commanded them to depart. I told them that the elders were under my protection and that they could not harm one hair of their heads. All stood aghast.... God was with me. He placed those words in my mouth, or I could not have spoken them. All was calm, instantly. That strong, ferocious body of men stood helpless before a weak, trembling, yet fearless girl. The ministers turned and asked the mob to leave and they dispersed with sullen faces, in fear and in shame, broken in pride and remorse in spirit.... Soon all was quiet. We had met and vanquished the enemy and were permitted to finish our meeting in peace."

Marie and her family came to Zion in 1854. She married Charles Guild in 1855 and lived out her days in Piedmont, Wyoming—a mighty woman in Zion, with a noble posterity.

Marie wrote the following in her biography:

> "This account is written for the benefit of you, my children, in order to show you that our Heavenly Father has had great love for His children upon the whole earth, in revealing the fullness of the Gospel to the prophet Joseph Smith.... I bear my testimony unto you and unto the whole world that God has

spoken to His prophet, Joseph Smith, and has revealed unto him the fullness of the Gospel."

Source:

https://www.familysearch.org/tree/person/memories/KWJY-L56

O Lord, Save Me

The trail was a dangerous environment in a multitude of ways. If it was not wolves and snakes, it was the hazards of heavy wagons and oxen. Many lives were lost to mishaps along the trail. David John, who crossed the plains in 1861, was part of the Homer Duncan Company. On August 7, 1861, not far from Fort Laramie, Wyoming, David John recorded:

> "Traveled 19 miles, camped on the "Platte" on the south bank. At dusk, it became my time [or turn] to herd the cattle that night, so we drove the herd across the "Platte" to the north side, there being good feed. I rode a horse through the river. Soon it became too deep for the horse, so he commenced swimming. When we got to the north bank of the river, the horse had to go up a steep side, and being quite wet, before the horse got quite up on the north side, he fell on his back perpendicularly, and lighted in the river below—myself on his back. In the struggle, I was thrown from the saddle. The horse swam towards the north side of the river and myself carried towards the south side. I was bewildered. I remember that I shouted, "O Lord, save me.""

> "The following morning, Captain Duncan says that he saw me in the river and understood the words I said. Now I will relate in words of soberness what transpired which no doubt cannot be believed unless the mind of the reader be inspired by the Spirit of God:

After I uttered the words "O Lord, save me," I found myself on the back of the horse, my left hand holding in the bridle and my right hand having hold in the mane. How I was taken there, I know not. I heard no sound. I saw no being, but by the power of God I was placed there, and so steep and unfathomable are the works of God, that this strange miracle took place unaccountable by myself. The horse swam down the river till we came to a good landing. I dismounted, being wet through. I put fire to a large dry tree, standing up, dried myself and got warm, and when the dawn of day appeared, I crossed the river to the camp, while the fire still was burning in the tree. I will here observe that this circumstance surpasses my understanding, but I confess that God made himself manifest."

Source:

https://history.churchofjesuschrist.org/overlandtravel/sources/4700/john-david-journals-1856-1908-reel-1-vol-1-253-64

One of the Three Nephites

George Washington Adair and his wife, Miriam Ann
Billingsley Adair, met during the great Mormon Exodus to
the west. Miriam dreamed one night:

> "That a young man would come riding up to their
> wagon on a white horse. She had told her sister of
> her dream and of course they laughed about it as
> young romantic girls would, so when the young
> man did come riding into camp on a white horse,
> the two girls nudged each other and wondered if
> this was really true. Yes . . . that was the man that
> Miriam married before they reached the valley."

They courted in pioneer trail fashion and were married on
May 6, 1846. They came on to the Salt Lake Valley and
about 1849-1850 were living in the area of Sugarhouse.

> "The snow was very deep but the fires had to be
> kept burning so [George] had gone off to replenish
> the woodpile. While he was away one of the
> children became very ill. [Miriam] did all she could
> for the child but the child continued to get worse so
> [Miriam] did as she always did when a crisis came,
> to get down on her knees and ask her Heavenly
> Father to send her aid. After doing all that her
> knowledge prompted her to do, she heard a knock
> at the door—on opening it there stood a man who
> asked her if she would like him to administer to her
> child. Never doubting that the answer to her prayer
> had come, she got the oil, which she always had on
> hand, and the man administered to her child. Her

attention was turned to the child for the moment so when she turned to thank him for coming, he had left without saying anything. She hurried to the door to see if she could call him to give her thanks, but there was no one in sight nor were there any foot steps or prints in the snow....Her child was healed and was perfectly well when her husband returned."

Miriam ever after believed that her timely and powerful visitor was one of the Three Nephites, and likely it may have been. There are angels among us.

Source:

From Miriam's history written by her granddaughter Ethel Adair Pope, October 1967.

https://www.familysearch.org/tree/person/memories/KWJ6-TJ8

11
Chapter Eleven

Patience's Angel

On October 29, 1856, the members of the Martin
Handcart Company were in a terrible state, starved,
freezing, and exhausted, with barely one-third able
to walk. Yet, moved by the hope that somewhere on
the road ahead wagons loaded with food and supplies
were waiting for them, they got up and began to move,
leaving behind 56 of their number who had died over
the previous ten days. They were in such dire straits
that it seemed impossible to move, but somehow,
notwithstanding the deep snow, they did. The Loader
family suffered along with the rest, having buried James
Loader back along the trail. On the day they left Red
Buttes Camp, near present-day Casper, Wyoming,
Patience recorded the following:

> "I will say we traveled on all day in the snow,
> but the weather was fine and in the middle
> of the day the sun was quite warm. Sometime
> in the afternoon, a strange man appeared to
> me as we were resting. As we got up the hill
> he came and looked in my face. He said, 'Are
> you Patience?' I said, 'Yes.' He said again, 'I
> thought it was you. Travel on, there is help
> for you. You will come to a good place and
> there is plenty.' With this, he was gone. He
> disappeared. I looked, but never saw where he
> went. This seemed very strange to me. I took
> this as someone sent to encourage us and give us
> strength."

That next day, Patience and the Martin Company met the relief wagons near Greasewood Creek, not far from Devil's Gate, Wyoming. The rescuers had a dozen large fires burning, food, clothing, and supplies to give a measure of relief and comfort.

The Martin Company in the depth of their ordeal may have wondered, as have many in the decades since, if God had forsaken them on the high plains of Wyoming, but it is my witness that heaven was watching— closely—and the plan and purposes of the Almighty were fulfilled to His glory and theirs. "Wherefore, by the ministering of angels...men begin to exercise faith in Christ" (Moroni 7:25).

Source:
Glenn Rawson, Journal of the Handcart Pioneers, History of the Saints, p. 130

12
Chapter Twelve

So Much Work Has to Be Done

The occasion was a church conference of the Weber Stake in Ogden, Utah, on Monday, October 19, 1896. The speaker was President Wilford Woodruff. In his talk, he spoke of angelic visitations from brethren he had known in this life. He spoke of a visit from Joseph and Hyrum Smith, while enroute to his last mission to England. He then said:

"Joseph Smith continued visiting myself and others up to a certain time, and then it stopped. The last time I saw him was in heaven. In the night vision, I saw him at the door of the temple in heaven. He came and spoke to me. He said he could not stop to talk with me because he was in a hurry. The next man I met was Father Smith; he could not talk with me because he was in a hurry. I met half a dozen brethren who had held high positions on earth, and none of them could stop to talk with me because they were in a hurry. I was much astonished. By and by, I saw the Prophet again, and I got the privilege to ask him a question. 'Now,' said I, 'I want to know why you are in a hurry. I have been in a hurry all through my life; but I expected my hurry would be over when I got into the Kingdom of Heaven, if I ever did.' Joseph said, 'I will tell you, Brother Woodruff. Every dispensation that has had the priesthood on the earth and has gone into the Celestial Kingdom, has had a certain amount of work to do to prepare to go to the earth with the Savior when He goes to reign on the earth. Each dispensation has had ample time to do this work. We have not. We are the last dispensation, and so much work has to be done, and we need to be in a hurry in order to accomplish it.' Of course, that was satisfactory to me, but it was new doctrine to me."

Source:
https://rsc.byu.edu/banner-gospel-wilford-woodruff/every-man-given-gift

13
Chapter Thirteen
There Stood a Big, Fat Steer

The Ellsworth handcart company left Florence, Nebraska on July 16, 1856. They had two hundred-eighty people, fifty-six handcarts, and four wagons. The wagons were for the purpose of hauling the company's supplies. Mary Ann Jones, age 19, was part of that company and recorded the following in her diary:

> "The Lord was with us by His Spirit, for although tired and foot sore, we could sing the songs of Zion as we went along. Some stomachs may recoil at a supper cooked with the water dug in a buffalo wallow and cooked with buffalo chips, but it tasted good to us. We came to an [immense] herd of buffalo. It seemed as if the whole prairie was moving. We waited for over an hour for them to cross the road so we could go on…. A very remarkable thing happened on the Platte River. One of the oxen died and Brother Ellsworth was asking the brethren what could be done. Could they put a cow in the team so we could go on? When one of the men said, 'Look, Brother Ellsworth, at that steer on the hill,' for there stood a big, fat steer looking at us. Brother Ellsworth said, 'The Lord has sent him to help us into the valley. Go and get him so we can move on.' They did so, and he worked as good as the others. When we got within two days' travel of Salt Lake, we met some teams sent out from the valley with provisions and to help us in. The next morning when the boys went

to round up the cattle to start, that steer was gone. They hunted for hours, but we never saw him again. He went as mysteriously as he came. Brother Ellsworth said the Lord lent him to us as long as we needed him."

Mary Ann went on and captured the intrepid spirit of those pioneers and why they made the arduous journey they did. She said:

"We had reached the goal and on foot all the way. I never left my handcart for a day and only rode over two rivers. We waded streams, crossed high mountains and pulled through heavy sands—leaving comfortable homes, fathers, mother, brothers and sisters—and what for? [We left] to be where we could hear a prophet's voice and live with the Saints of God. I have never seen the day I regretted my trip. We arrived in Salt Lake on the 26th day of September, 1856."

We live in a day when we can hear the voice of a prophet. What are we willing to do to hear a prophet and live with the Saints of God?

Source:
*https://history.churchofjesuschrist.org/overlandtravel/pioneers/18472/
mary-ann-jones*

14
Chapter Fourteen
What Book Is That

It was November 11, 1837, in Far West, Missouri. Benjamin Benson, in an interview, shared the following story with Joseph Smith, the Prophet.

The year was 1795. At that time, Benjamin was 22 years old and living in the town of Pompey, New York. Benjamin saw in the area where he lived, evidence of the ancient indigenous peoples of the Americas. He said:

> "My mind was anxiously led to contemplate and reflect on where those Indians came from, or from what race of people they sprang from.... I firmly believing that the Bible was true, my heart's desire was to God in solemn prayer to know where and what race of people these Indians sprang from."

After making it a matter of earnest prayer for several days, Benjamin shared the following with Joseph:

> "An angel, as I thought, came to me and said, 'Come along with me,' and I was immediately on a beast like a horse, and the angel at my left hand, with his feet about the same height that my feet were as I sat on the horse, and in this position was conveyed to near the place where the record was deposited, and he said, 'stop here'; and the angel went about four or five rods and took in his hand a book, and on his return

to where I stood, as I thought, there were many stood with me.

One said, 'What book is that?' and the answer was, it is a bible, a bible, the word of God, a record of a people that came from Jerusalem, the forefathers of these Indians; and it also contains a record of a people that came from the Tower of Babel at the time the Lord confounded the language and scattered the people into all the world, and it, the Book of Ether. And then, with great anxiety of heart, I asked if I might have the book, and [the] answer was that it was not the Lord's time then, but it should come, 'and you shall see it.' And then said, 'Look,' and as I looked, I beheld a man standing, as I thought at a distance of two hundred yards, and the angel said 'there is the man that the Lord hath appointed…and he is not yet born.'"

So—Benjamin Benson was taken to the Hill Cumorah, where he saw the book that would come forth of the gold plates and was given to understand that the people who buried that record came from Jerusalem. He also saw the man who would bring forth that record— Joseph Smith Jr.—who would not be born for another ten years.

Benjamin saw the vision in 1795. He was introduced to and joined the church with his family in 1832, in Indiana. In 1837, forty-two years after the vision, he shared it with the Prophet Joseph Smith on November 11, 1837. At the Prophet's request, Benjamin gave an abbreviated account of the vision in a letter, dated November 12, 1837. That letter was subsequently copied into Joseph Smith's Letter Book and is

referenced here. Benjamin Benson died in 1846, during the saint's journey to the Rocky Mountains.

How many witnesses are there to the truthfulness and divine origins of the Book of Mormon? Innumerable! How many is it going to take to convince this world that the record is true and Jesus is the Christ?

Source:

https://www.josephsmithpapers.org/paper-summary/letter-from-benjamin-benson-12-november-1837/1#source-note

https://www.familysearch.org/tree/person/memories/KWVS-7V7

You Shall Go to That City

Louis Frederick Moench was born in Neuffen, Germany in 1846, the eleventh child of fourteen children born to Johann Christian and Elizabeth Barbara Moench. The family was very poor, which was the reason that in 1852, Christian left for America. He established himself as a tanner near Gowanda, New York and sent for two of his older children. He would never return to Germany.

In his absence, [his] mother, Barbara Hess Moench, struggled mightily to provide for her children. Though the necessities of life were scarce and hard to obtain, the singing of hymns and reading of scriptures were a guided staple for the family. Later, Barbara became ill and slowly began to waste away. When finally she was confined to her bed, her son Louis would sit by her side and read the Bible to her. Her granddaughter wrote of those days:

> "During those long, sad days, she received her greatest comfort from her Lutheran Bible which Louis spent all of his leisure hours reading to her. Though only nine years old, he was an excellent reader, with a voice rich and musical, soothing to the dying woman. It was reading at his mother's bedside that gave him a literary training which something about the rhapsody of Isaiah, which particularly appealed to him in his reading one day:

"Awake, awake; put on thy strength, O Zion; put on thy beautiful garments, O Jerusalem, the holy city, for henceforth there shall no more come unto thee the uncircumcised and the unclean." On he read: "How beautiful upon the mountains are the feet of him that bringeth good tidings that publisheth peace... that saith unto Zion, thy God reigneth! ...for they shall see eye to eye, when the Lord shall bring again Zion."

The Bible was laid down and the boy asked; "Mother, what is meant by this 'Zion' of which Isaiah, the prophet, speaks so much?" [She replied,] "It is a peaceful, beautiful city that will be in the last days." [I asked,] "Will I ever go to that city, Mother?" [She answered,] 'My son, I promise that if you will always live as I have taught you, you shall go to that city.'"

In January 1856, Louis's dear mother passed away and just two weeks later, his brother Willie joined her. Shortly after, Louis and the remaining children emigrated to America and joined their father and siblings. Louis' father decreed that he had received enough schooling and was to join him in the tannery. However, at the age of eighteen, Louis went to Chicago, where with hard work, determination, and night school, Louis excelled and graduated from Bryant Stratton College.

In 1864, Louis set out with a friend to cross the United States to California, where the two young men would pursue the occupation of teachers. They had a single wagon filled with supplies and two mules. By early August, 1864, they had crossed Wyoming and came down into the canyons of Utah. They camped and enjoyed a

good trout breakfast. The mountain air and abundant wildlife caused them to decide to lay over one more day in search of game.

Louis's traveling companion, Henry Trescott, observed that they were not more than fifty miles out of Salt Lake City, to which Louis responded, "We must make an early start tomorrow morning, for I will never spend a night in Salt Lake City."

[Henry said,] "You are very much prejudiced against the Mormons, Louis. I don't care to have much to do with them myself, but those we have met seem to be hard working, honest people."

[Louis replied,] "Oh, yes, that is true enough, but I have no use for their religion. I don't want their polygamy, and I don't want their golden Bible. I repeat, I will not spend a night in Salt Lake City."

They spent the day hunting for game. As they returned to their wagon, they were dismayed to observe that a mountain breeze had fanned their campfire into a blaze and sent sparks into their wagon. Everything but the clothes on their backs was ash.

"Looks like you're staying in Salt Lake more than one night, Louis," commented Henry Trescott.

"I suppose we'll stay there with the Mormons until we can get another outfit," replied Louis. "We cannot go on to California without."

They made their way into the city, where they found lodging with a motherly midwife named Almeda Farr. She made them welcome and they stayed. She became like a mother to Louis and in time he was "perfectly at home in her house." She gave him a copy of the Book of Mormon, which he studied, marked, and prayed about. He came to know it was the word of God. Thus it was, that on fast day, February 6, 1867, Louis Frederick Moench was baptized.

> "That night, as he laid upon his bed, a light entered his room, and he saw his mother standing by his bed. Little Willie was holding her hand. The smile that she gave him made him know that the step he had taken had met with her approval and her dying promise had been fulfilled. He had lived to come to Zion."

Sources:

https://www.familysearch.org/tree/person/memories/LKVY-CSP

https://contentdm.lib.byu.edu/digital/collection/BYUIBooks/id/3624

A Very Strange Blessing

It was on June 5, 1838, that the Alfred Bosworth Child family was baptized in St. Lawrence County, New York. George Blakely was the elder who taught and baptized them. On August 11 of that same year, the family began the journey to join the saints in Kirtland, Ohio. It was while traveling through the heavy forests of eastern Ohio, that the following experience occurred.

The Child family was in the lead wagon. Two other families were following behind. The canvas wagon sides were rolled up and all the family rode in the wagon, enjoying the sights and sounds as they journeyed. Suddenly, a voice was heard, "Whoa!" Alfred, who was sitting in the front, looked around, but no one was in the vicinity. The Child team stopped so abruptly that the team following behind made contact with the Child's wagon. Then, according the account written by Warren Gould Child, who was there:

> "A personage walked unconcernedly up to the wagon. He had the appearance of being very aged, well dressed, with an unusual long white beard, tidy in his appearance from head to foot, apparently about six feet tall, of rather spare build, carrying a very pleasant and happy look on his face. He asked no questions as to who we were or where we were going, but proceeded to shake hands with the family, commencing with Father first, then Mother, and each of the children according to age, blessing them in the

name of Jesus Christ, the writer being the next to youngest in the family at that time.

After getting through in this manner, he turned to me the second time and pronounced a further and special blessing, placing his hand on my bare head. Without further words, he slowly passed on. The visit was so sudden and unlooked for that not a word [was] spoken by the family. Father expected he would do likewise with the families occupying the two wagons behind us, but he simply made a slight bow as he passed them. Some of the families got out to hail him and get a further explanation of so strange and unlooked for occurrence.

They went quickly to the rear, and to their surprise, he was nowhere to be seen. They made a hasty search in every direction, but he was nowhere to be found. Search in each direction was made in the road for his tracks, but none were anywhere to be found. The families traveling with us remarked that we had received a very strange blessing from a stranger. On arriving in Kirtland, Father related the occurrence to the Prophet Joseph Smith, [who] told him that the personage was none other than one of the Nephites who were permitted not to taste death, and that they made occasional visits where they were permitted."

Source:
https://www.familysearch.org/tree/person/memories/KWJY-B3N

17
Chapter Seventeen
Don't Cry My Little Dears

Joseph Ainsworth and his wife Mary joined The Church of Jesus Christ of Latter-day Saints in England, during the first mission of Heber C. Kimball, in 1837. On July 4, 1854, a daughter, Mary Jane, was born, bringing the family to five. When Mary Jane was only two years old, her father passed away. Then, in 1862, the family sailed to America on the steamship Manchester. There was Mary Jane, her mother, and her two older brothers, Joseph and James. They landed at Castle Gardens, New York and then made their way to Florence, Nebraska, where they joined up with the Henry Miller wagon company. Mary Jane's mother was ill the entirety of the voyage across the sea, and was still not well as they began their journey across the plains on August 5, 1862.

One day, somewhere along the trail, it was late in the day and almost time for the company to make camp. Mary Jane and her brother went out to gather buffalo chips for their evening cook fire. Mary Jane and her brother were so intent on their work that they wandered out some distance from the road and failed to notice the train move on. They quickly became lost as the darkness closed in upon them. Their terror was even more as the wolves began to howl all around them. They were far out away from civilization, with no one to help them.

Remembering what their mother had taught them, they knelt down and asked Heavenly Father to "keep

them from harm and to guide them safely to where the company was camped."

According to the family history:

> "Soon after this, they saw an old lady who said to them, "Don't cry my little dears, I'll take you to the camp; follow me." She was not a member of their camp and when she had led them nearly to their camp, she disappeared."

When the children related the experience to their mother, she told them the old lady was surely an angel sent to help them. "And who can doubt that mother's word, for what mortal being would there be on that trackless waste so far from human habitation alone at night?"

Mary Jane and her family came on safely to the Salt Lake Valley. Her mother remarried in 1865. Then, one year later, Mary Jane's stepfather was injured and died a few days later.

On the same day that he died, their wheat stacks, hay, and everything they had, burned to the ground. The shock of losing everything they had, and her husband's death, was too much for the already weakened body of the little mother and she died a week later. She passed to her final rest in October 1866. Her last words to her daughter [Mary Jane] were, "My dear, never leave the Gospel. It is true and I want to meet you on the other side."

Mary Jane never left the gospel. She became the mother of ten children, a nurse, a primary president for twenty years, and faithful daughter of God. She is buried in Brigham City, Utah.

Source:

https://www.familysearch.org/tree/person/memories/KWJD-JGD

Get My Servant

In December 1853, Canute Peterson was serving as a missionary in his native land of Norway. Under the direction of his mission president, he set sail with nearly seventy saints in a little vessel captained by a man named Thoresen. Upon arriving in Copenhagen, they were shown to a rented hall for their accommodations. Elder Peterson learned that he was to return to Christiania, his field of labor, but since the harbor was closed to shipping because of ice, he would have to walk hundreds of miles through deep snow across Sweden—a most discouraging idea. "The thoughts of this journey made me feel very low-spirited indeed," he said, "and I went down to the hall where the Saints were staying to try to cheer up."

About nine o'clock that evening, he felt a heavy hand strike him on the shoulder from behind. He turned around and, to his great surprise, it was Captain Thoresen. "Why, Captain Thoreson, are you here?" I said.

Captain Thoresen explained, "I came for you; I want you to go back to Norway with me, and right away with the returning train to Roskilla. I have a cab outside now waiting for us."

Elder Peterson was overjoyed at the prospect of not having to walk and he quickly gathered his things and went with the captain. As they journeyed, Captain Thoresen explained his presence.

"The next morning after you and your company
had left me at Holmbeck," he said, "I was
lying in my berth, and drawing the curtain
aside. I looked out into the cabin; to my great
astonishment, I saw a very fine-looking man
standing before me. He was dressed in white,
and his clothes were of peculiar fashion. He
called me by name and said: 'Go to Copenhagen
and get my servant, Canute Peterson, and
take him back with you to Norway.' He then
disappeared.

"Coming on deck, my brother, the mate,
noticing that I was nervous and pale, asked what
had happened. I told him what I had seen, and
the command of my strange visitor. 'Pshaw! that
was only a dream,' answered my brother. 'We
have no time for that; if you go to Copenhagen,
it means that we must remain here longer; we
will get frozen in, and then we will have to
stay here all winter and lose more than we have
made. No, we must hurry and buy up our cargo,
and get out of this firth right away.'"

The Captain continued:

"We tried to buy up our cargo that day, but
were unsuccessful. When I retired that night, I
could not help wondering whether that person
would again appear to me or not. The next
morning when I awoke, it was broad daylight,
and I hastened to dress myself. While sitting on
the edge of the berth to put on my stockings,
I looked up and there stood before me that
same person. He raised his hand, and pointing
to me, said: 'Captain Thoreson, if you do not

go to Copenhagen and get my servant, Canute Peterson, to go back with you to Norway, you will surely be wrecked and lose your life.' Then he vanished. I hastened on deck, and again related to my brother the strange circumstance. 'Well,' said he, 'perhaps you had better go to Copenhagen and get Peterson.' Then it was agreed that he should load up the vessel as soon as possible. and sail out to the open sea, and I was to go to Copenhagen to get you."

With that explanation, Captain Thoresen and Elder Peterson arrived in Holmbeck and arranged for a boat to take them out to the ship. Once onboard, they continued sailing toward Norway, staying in sight of the shore. At one point, the winds turned contrary and were driving them dangerously close to shore. Elder Canute Peterson continued the narrative:

"We soon found that we were in great danger of being dashed to pieces. Realizing our extreme danger, I went down into the cabin and tried to offer up a word of prayer. I came up on deck and still our position was very perilous. After a few moments, I returned to pray again, and this time my prayer was answered. When I came on deck, the Captain, being fully aware that I had been praying, said: 'This time your prayer was heard, for see, the wind is coming from the shore.' A very favorable breeze now helped us to pass this dangerous point, and we sailed on toward our destination without further danger or delay. When everything became pleasant, the Captain said: 'Now I can see where the danger was, and, I think, where my grave would have been, if I had disobeyed.'"

 47

Source:

https://www.familysearch.org/tree/person/memories/KWJC-WRV

He Was Truly Beautiful

My friend, Carol Judd, shared with me a most remarkable experience. It came at a time when she was serving as a police officer at the Port of Entry. It happened in June 1997. She and another female officer were traveling to a meeting in Phoenix. It was early in the morning, between 5:30-6:00 a.m. They were just past the Tuba City Junction, Arizona when they came upon a car accident. They were the first on the scene. She gave the following details:

> "There were two Navajo men, a father and a son. The son was about 25 or 30. The father had a very bad head injury, and it was pretty obvious he was not going to make it. The son was banged up pretty bad, but he was going to be alright. We tried everything we could for the father. [We] cleaned him up the best we could while waiting on the ambulance. Then, out of nowhere, a very tall Navajo man, who was beautifully dressed in starched jeans with a white, starched, long-sleeved shirt, appeared at the scene. He was wearing a beautiful old turquoise Navajo concho belt, an old turquoise squash blossom necklace, and big, old, turquoise bracelets. His hair was long, black, and was very carefully groomed into braids…. [He] was impeccably dressed, almost military in appearance. He walked over to the dying man, knelt down, put his hands on his head, and gave him a blessing to be released from this

life. He never spoke to me or the other officer, but as quick as he came, he got into a car and left, having never spoken a word to either of us. I knew that something special was going on because of the immense feeling of peace that was there at that moment. The man himself was someone very special. I never have seen anything like him before or since. He was truly beautiful."

Was this wonderful priesthood man mortal or immortal? I don't know. It does not matter. He was at the moment a ministering messenger, an angel sent from God.

Source:
Experience of Carol Judd

His Conduct Was Above Question

"It was a cold night in the latter part of November, and in the home of William Huntington. The family gathered around the big fireplace in the spacious kitchen. After the evening meal, when all the evening work was done, it was the habit of this family to get their instruments of music and sit around the blazing logs and play the old fashioned tunes and hymns, also tunes of more cheerful air, although they did not dance. Grandfather Huntington played the bass viol, his daughter Zina the cello, William, the cornet, and Dimick, the drum. There were five sons and two daughters, the oldest daughter, Presenda, being married, lived some distance from them. It was a happy New England family and they lived the clean, pure life of the Puritan stock. After the music ceased, a hush fell on the group and a knock was heard on the door and as it opened, a strange old gentleman of medium weight, dressed in old-fashioned clothes and carrying a bundle on his arm, appeared and stepped into the room and said: 'I usually bend my steps to some sequestered vale. May I find lodging here tonight?'

"With cordial welcome, he was invited in and given a place by the fire, in an old easy farm chair, and mother Huntington asked if he would like some supper and modestly he said he would.

Then a good New England meal was spread before him, with milk, honey, maple syrup, cold meat, and delicious homemade bread and butter. He partook of a light supper while the family spoke in soft tones. It was the custom to read a portion of the scriptures before going to bed. He again joined the circle, and father Huntington began to read from the Holy Bible, a portion of the New Testament, to which they all listened attentively. Grandmother Huntington made some comment on the fact that they would like to hear the gospel in its fullness as explained and taught by the Saviour. The stranger immediately took up the subject and began explaining the scriptures and quoting the sayings of the Saviour in what seemed to them a new light and greater beauty than they had ever thought of before.

"They sat in rapt attention, listening to every word. Both father and mother Huntington agreed with his explanations, while the boys exchanged glances of admiration and the daughter, Zina, was spellbound and sat and gazed upon the stranger with admiration and reverence. After one hour spent in conversation upon this sacred subject, Father Huntington had prayers, Mother Huntington prepared a comfortable resting place for the stranger, and he bid them good night. The boys [were] going upstairs, Father and Mother Huntington to their bedroom which led from the kitchen, and Zina in her little bed heard her parents talking in low tones about the wonderful stranger and discussing the things he said. The stranger had filled them with awe and reverence, such as they had never felt before. In the morning, everyone

was astir bright and early as is usual on a farm when so much work has to be done, both outside and in."

"The stranger sat placidly watching the remarkable family with whom he took breakfast. The family invited him to stay, but he said he had other places to visit and he left them standing in a group as he closed the door softly. When Father Huntington saw the stranger depart, he sent Dimick after him to tell him to come again. He immediately opened the door and they all looked out to see and call the stranger back, but he was nowhere to be seen. When looking on the doorstep where the snow had fallen the night before, no trace of a footstep could be seen and the boys running from all directions said that he had vanished and could not be found. Father Huntington remarked that he was the strangest person that ever was and he could not understand where he went, but he had shown them the gospel in a new light."

"Mother Huntington felt that this stranger was some messenger from heaven and all the family were deeply impressed with his wonderful influence and beautiful way of explaining the scriptures."

"When the gospel to life and salvation was brought to them by Hyrum Smith and other Elders, they seemed to coincide with what the stranger had told them concerning the Bible and the restoration of the gospel. All the family but one accepted the gospel and prepared to emigrate in a few years to Kirtland; here they met the

Prophet of God, Joseph Smith, and became his faithful and loyal followers and friends.

Source:
Zina Young Card, "Zina Diantha Huntington Young," copy of typescript, Zina D. H. Young collection.

Additional sources tell more of the life of William Huntington.

> "On an occasion when the Prophet Joseph was speaking of the three Nephites, Brother Huntington related this little incident to him. He laid his hand on his head and said: 'My dear brother, that man was one of the three Nephites who came to prepare you for the restoration of the Gospel and its acceptance.'"

Source:
William Huntington, Autobiography, 1.

Of the revered patriarch of that family, William Huntington let me continue. He took his family and joined The Church of Jesus Christ of Latter-day Saints. Where the church went, William followed. All that the members suffered, sacrificed and endured. He was there. In July of 1839, when so many were sick and dying in Nauvoo, his wife Zina passed away at the age of 53. In August of 1840, William married Lydia Clisbee Partridge, the widow of Edward Partridge.

William struggled with his health and labored to build the Nauvoo temple all the while. When the church went west in 1846, William was appointed captain of over 100 families. The crossing of Iowa was terrible. The weather, mud, snow, and sickness made it unbearable and tedious.

William and company got as far as present-day Mt. Pisgah, Iowa when President Young asked William and his company to stay and build the settlement up. Then, in his journal dated June 1846, William recorded this:

> "I am appointed to preside over the portion of [the] Church that stopped here (Mount Pisgah). We are building fences and plowing. The brethren are coming in hourly. The U.S. [Army is] calling up 500 men to engage in war with Mexico."

William literally wasted and wore out his life in love and service at Pisgah. It is said:

> "He labored extremely hard and tirelessly to comfort the sick and look after the general welfare of the people left here. He was beloved by the Saints, for he was a true friend and brother to all, and his conduct was above question. On Aug 9, 1845 he was taken sick with chills and fever of which he died August 19, 1846.

William Huntington was true and faithful to the very end. Like so many, he never lived to see the saints established in these mountains.

Source:
https://www.familysearch.org/tree/person/memories/KWV9-4W1

21
Chapter Twenty-One
I Saw the Angels

The following story is from the "History of Zerah Pulsipher" (1789-1872), as written by him.

"When I was about twenty-one, I married a very agreeable companion, lived with her for about one year ,when she died leaving one child which we named Harriet. After the death of my wife, [called] Polly or Mary Randell, I had some anxiety about her state and condition. Consequently, in answer to my desires, in a few weeks she came to me in vision, and appearing natural, looked pleasant as she ever did, sat by my side and assisted me in singing a hymn-— beginning thus: 'That glorious day is drawing nigh, when Zions Light Shall Shine.' This she did with a seeming composure. This vision took away all the anxiety of my mind concerning her, in as much as she seemed to enjoy herself well."

Zerah would later learn of the hymn's greater meaning when he learned of the Restored Gospel of Jesus Christ, but for the time, he said, "My mind became calm as respecting her condition in the Spirit World."

Zerah married again and moved to New York state. It was there, in 1831, that he first heard mention of the Book of Mormon. Not long after, he obtained a copy of the book and read it through twice. He heard Elder Jared Carter declare it to be "a revelation from God." Hearing that, Zerah said:

"I was determined to have that knowledge for myself, which I considered it my privilege. From that time, I made it a matter of fervent prayer. I think about the seventh day, as I was thrashing in my barn with doors shut, all at once there seemed to be a ray of light from heaven which caused me to stop work for a short time—but soon began again. Then, in a few minutes, another light came over my head, which caused me to look up. I thought I saw the Angels with the Book of Mormon in their hands, in the attitude of showing it to me and saying, 'This is the Great Revelation of the Last Days in which all things spoken of by the Prophets must be fulfilled.' The vision was so open and plain that I began to rejoice exceedingly so that I walked the length of my barn crying, 'Glory Hal-La-Lu-Ya to the God and the Lamb forever.' For some time, it seemed a little difficult to keep my mind in a proper state of reasonable order. I was filled with the joys of heaven."

Zerah Pulsipher was baptized and gathered with the Saints. He served multiple missions. One of those who heard him preach and was baptized was Wilford Woodruff. He emigrated to Utah and lived out his days in southern Utah and served as a patriarch up to the time of his passing. In the spring of 1870, Zerah "had a severe fit of sickness, which came very near to taking him away." During this time, "he saw a vision—Elder Kimball, who had died a few months before, in a carriage more beautiful than is known on earth, called him to jump in and go along with them. He was informed that he had worked too hard and had not taken proper care of himself. He was about to go [die]". Zerah's son William's "faith, prayers, and administrations prevailed with the

Lord " and he was permitted to live with his family almost two more years. He died on January 1, 1872, at the age of 82.

Source:

http://www.johnpratt.com/gen/8/z_pulsipher.html

https://ancestors.familysearch.org/en/K2HH-5XK/zerah pulsipher-1789-1872

https://www.josephsmithpapers.org/person/zera-pulsipher

22
Chapter Twenty-Two

I Won't Have Your Place

The year was 1835 near Albion, Illinois. Two men, Jefferson Hunt and John Woodland, attended a meeting in which they first heard the restored gospel of Jesus Christ preached. The following was recorded in Woodland family records:

> [They were] "told of the heavenly visitations of a messenger and that Joseph Smith had obtained some marvelous records. It was a very strange story. After leaving the meeting and bidding good night to Jefferson Hunt, John was impressed to pray. The evil one tried to overcome him, but he cast it off. John became thoroughly satisfied that the gospel was true. Through this testimony, he said all his family and Jefferson Hunt were baptized."

After joining the church, Jefferson Hunt wanted to sell out and join the Saints in Missouri. John purchased his friend's farm. That night, after the purchase, an angel of the Lord appeared to John in a dream and showed him a beautiful piece of land, his new home, and told him to go and search it out. He was told that he would know the place by a grove of trees in which a single tree would stand much higher than the others. He was to go to that tree, "place his back against it" and pace off to the west. "There he would find a spring with white sand boiling up in it, and he would know that this was his new home."

The next morning, John told Jefferson Hunt about the dream and asked if he would wait a few days and he would go with him to Missouri. Not long after, the two men saddled up and rode into Missouri. Jefferson Hunt soon found a place that suited him and laid his claim. John felt impressed to turn to the north. They rode about two miles and saw a grove of trees with one standing higher than the rest. "There is the tree I saw in my dream," exclaimed John. They rode into the grove. John placed his back against the tree and walked 25 paces west and there found the white sand spring he had seen in vision. It was a beautiful place. John built a cabin to lay his claim and the two men went back to Illinois to get their families.

In 1838, the Prophet Joseph Smith came to visit John and Celia Woodland at their home in Daviess County Missouri. The records say:

> "After looking over the place, he said: 'Oh, Brother John, what a pretty place you have! What would you take for it for a Stake in Zion?' Brother Woodland answered: 'If it is the will of the Lord, take it and give me another place as good.' Brother Joseph stood a minute, bowed his head, and after standing in this attitude for some minutes, raised his head and said: 'Brother John, I won't have your place, for the Lord showed it to you and you had faith enough to seek it out.' He then placed his hands on Brother Woodland's head and sealed the place unto him and his posterity for life and all eternity. He told him to never sell the place. John was afterward offered a great amount of money for it, but would not sell it and forbade his posterity

to ever sell it. This place is on Spring Hill, very near to Adam-ondi-Ahman."

John and Celia Woodland lived on that property until mob violence and the Extermination Order of the Governor drove them out. Their house was burned, their property destroyed, and family members murdered, but the Woodlands kept the faith and followed the church to Nauvoo and later to Utah. They were both laid to rest in the old cemetery in Willard, Utah.

Source:

https://www.familysearch.org/tree/person/memories/KWJB-JL7

23
Chapter Twenty-Three
It Was Absolutely Real

Steven Crofts was called to serve in the Sweden, Stockholm mission in 1973. While he was in training at then, Ricks College in Rexburg, he received word that his grandfather had passed away. This was extremely hard on him. He describes the relationship he had with "Papa."

> "For almost all of my life before my mission, I had lived two blocks away from my Papa and Grandma Crofts. I was their first grandson. Papa was a lumberman and worked in the timber industry in southern Utah. He was not the kind of man who liked to sit behind a desk. He did a lot of traveling around and often took me with him, especially in the summer. We did a lot of hunting and fishing and all kinds of exploring, mostly in southern Utah. Twice during the summertime, he took me to Canada to his lumber operations in British Columbia. I loved him beyond what words can describe. He was absolutely a hero to me. I was extremely close to him. I actually wrote a book about all the life lessons I learned from him."

Elder Crofts chose not to attend the funeral, but stay on his mission and work even harder.

Later, after he had been in Sweden a few months, he attended his first Zone Conference in Stockholm. That night, after the first day of meetings, they went back to

where they were staying with a member family. They were exhausted and went to bed. Elder Crofts tells of a most sacred dream he received that night:

> "In the middle of the night, I sat up in bed, and to this day I can remember, like it was yesterday, the dream that just occurred. In the dream, Papa and I were sitting in big comfortable chairs in a beautiful room, seated across from each other. He told me to not be worried about my mission and my family at home and to just work hard and be a great missionary. He told me he was proud of me and was excited that I'd been called to Europe. As a footnote, he had served in Germany and my father served in the Netherlands. He then stood up, walked over to me, and put his hands on my head. He blessed me to work hard and that if I did, I would be a successful missionary and that great opportunities to serve would open up to me. He blessed me with a command of the language. He then blessed me that my health would be good and that it would not be an issue for me at all during my mission. And then, all of a sudden, it was over, and I woke up sitting up in my sleeping bag. It was absolutely real. I sat there amazed for a long time and decided I would write the story in my journal later in the day and send the story to my grandmother."

There is greater significance to the blessing of health than is readily apparent. Steven had suffered with severe ulcers since the age of 13. At one point, it had even bled considerably, a fact he did not reveal to his family or doctor in preparing for his mission. He went into the mission field still in misery, wondering if he would be able to get through two years. He continues:

"After his blessing, I did not have any more ulcer issues during my entire mission—not a single bit of pain or other side effects. To me, it was a miracle."

Steven completed his mission and enjoyed many wonderful experiences. Shortly after he returned home, the ulcers returned, perforated the lining of his stomach, and at the tender age of 22, Steven was rushed into emergency surgery. That surgery was successful and Steven's ulcers never returned.

Source:

Contributed by Steven Crofts

24
Chapter Twenty-Four

Oh, You Beautiful Child

"I have been requested to relate an experience I had in 1908 or 1909 in San Juan County. I was just making a home in Blanding, and the whole county there was covered with trees and sagebrush. I was working hard to clear the ground to plant a few acres of corn. We had five acres cleared and we started to plant the corn. My little boy, Roy, age seven or eight years old, was there to help me plant the corn. I'd plow around the piece and then he'd plant the furrow with the corn. Then I'd cover it, and plow again. While I was plowing on that piece of ground, I discovered there were ancient houses there, that is, the remnants of them.

As I was plowing around, I noticed that my plow had turned out to be the skeleton of a small child—the skull and the backbone. Most of the bones, of course, were decayed and gone. Part of the skeleton was there, so I stopped immediately as my plow had passed it a little. I turned and looked back against the bar of the plow between the handles. As I was looking at that little skeleton that I had plowed out, and wondering, all of a sudden to my surprise, I saw the bones begin to wiggle. They began to change position and to take on a different color. Within a minute, there lay a beautiful little skeleton. It was a perfect little skeleton.

Then I saw the inner parts of the natural body coming in—the entrails, etc. I saw the flesh coming on and I saw the skin come on the body after the inner parts of the body were complete. A beautiful head of hair adorned the top of the head. In about a half a minute after the hair was on the head, it had a beautiful crystal decoration in the hair. It was combed beautifully and parted on one side. In about a half a minute after the hair was on the head, the child raised up on her feet. She was lying a little on her left side with her back toward me. Because of this, I wasn't able to discern the sex of the child, but as she raised up, a beautiful robe came down over her left shoulder and I saw it must be a girl.

She looked at me and I looked at her, and for a quarter of a minute we just looked at each other smiling. Then, in my ambition to get a hold of her, I said, "Oh, you beautiful child," and I reached out as if I would embrace her and she disappeared.

That was all I saw, and I stood there and I wondered and I thought for a few minutes. My little boy was wondering why I was there because he was down at the other end of the row, anxious to come and plant the corn. Now, I couldn't tell that story to anyone because it was so mysterious to me and such. Why should I have such a miraculous experience? I couldn't feature a human being in such a condition as to accidentally plow that little body out and see it come alive. A body of a child about five to seven years old, I'd say.

I couldn't tell that story to anyone until finally one day I met a dear friend of mine, Stake Patriarch Wayne H. Redd, of Blanding. He stopped me on the street and said, 'Zeke, you have had an experience on this mesa you won't tell. I want you to tell it to me.' Well, I told it to him. Then he had me tell it to other friends and since then I have told it in four temples in the United

States and many meeting houses and many socials, fast meetings, and at conference times.

I wondered, and it worried me for years, as to why…was I, just a common uneducated man, allowed to see such a marvelous manifestation of God's power.

One day, as I was walking alone with my hoe on my shoulder, going to hoe some corn, something said, 'Stop under the shade of that tree for a few minutes and rest.' This just came to me and I thought I would, so I stopped there and the following was given to me. It was in answer to my prayer. I prayed incessantly for an answer as to why I was privileged to see that resurrection. I was told why. When the child was buried there, it was either in time of war with the different tribes or it was winter time when the ground was frozen and they had no tools to dig deep graves. If it were during time of war, they couldn't possibly take time to dig a deep grave. They just planted that little body as deep as they could under the circumstances.

When it was done, the sorrowing mother knew that it was such a shallow grave, that in her sorrow she cried out to the little group that was present, 'That little shallow grave, the first beast that comes along will smell her body and will dig her up and scatter her to the four winds. Her bones will be scattered all over these flats.' There just happened to be a man present holding the priesthood (a Nephite or a Jaredite, I don't know which because they had both been in this country. I've been in their houses and know it.) The man said, 'Sister, calm your sorrows. Whenever that little body is disturbed or uncovered, the Lord will call her up and she will live.'

Since that time, I have taken great comfort, great cheer and consolation, and satisfaction, with praise in my heart and soul, until I haven't the words to express it, that it was I that uncovered that little body.

Thank you for listening to me. I just can't tell this without crying."

Source:
Contributed by Zeke Johnson, son of Joel Hills Johnson.

Relax, You Will Be Okay

One September night, in February 1970, Richard Burrows was on his way home to Provo, Utah. He had been in Salt Lake City, spending time with his future wife, Maureen, and her mother. Maureen's father had passed less than two years before. In those days, the freeway between Salt Lake City and Provo was still being built. That stretch of the road, known as "The Point of the Mountain", was under construction and, as so often happened, changed in layout almost daily. Richard was driving a Volkswagen Beetle at the time. Suddenly, the road curved, but all the markers and signs had blown down, and Richard found himself off the road and in the barrow pit. He describes what happened next:

> "As I hit this dirt, going about 75 miles per hour, a voice came to me and said, 'Relax, you will be ok.' I tried to get back on the road, and one of the bumpers hit a reflector post. My car spun and then started to roll. It rolled five times before coming to a stop in the mud and water in the middle of the highway. I saw the sky and the ground five times. Both doors had been ripped open. During those few seconds, I felt someone hold me down. I found myself upside down on the passenger floor. Back then there were no seatbelts. When I got out of the car, the roof of the car was crushed down and had smashed the tops of the seats. I was held in that car even without a seat belt and did not get ejected

through the open doors. Other than a small chip
on a bone in my ankle, caused by ripping out
the steering wheel, and a lot of bruises, I was
okay.

Richard did not recognize the voice that had protected
him, that is, until a few weeks later when listening to a
recording of Maureen's deceased father. It was the same
voice that had told him to relax.

The angels watch over us and miracles still happen.

Source:
Richard Burrows.

26

She Was Wearing a Dark Silk Dress

The year was 1858. Rumors reached the missionaries serving in New South Wales, Australia of a large army coming to Utah to wage war against the members of The Church of Jesus Christ of Latter-day Saints. The missionaries began departing Australia to return home. The President of the mission, Andrew Jackson Stewart, had heard nothing from Church Headquarters and decided to stay, even though his wife and family were living in Utah. In a letter written April 10, 1858, President Stewart wrote:

> "Since our last Conference in January, the times have been very dull, and great opposition to the work has been manifested in Australia. The attention of almost everyone has been turned to the "Mormon War." Some say they ought to be all killed off. Others are waiting to see the result; and if the Saints are not all killed off, they will come out on the Lord's side."

Shortly after that letter, President Stewart and another missionary, Amasa Potter, were sitting in the mission office in Sydney talking, when the door opened and in walked President Stewart's beloved wife, Eunice. "She was wearing a dark silk dress." Greetings were exchanged and then Eunice faced her husband and said, "Jackson, your release from your mission has come on the boat that has just come in the harbor." And with that, "Eunice disappeared as silently and quietly as she had entered." President Stewart went down to the post

office and there indeed was the letter, having just come in by ship. Both President Stewart and Elder Potter would attest to the visit of Eunice Stewart.

They later learned that at that very moment, on the other side of the world in Provo, Utah, Eunice Pease Quimby Stewart lay in a coma. "When she gained consciousness, she told her children that she had been to Australia and had seen and talked to her husband. She said that he had been released from his mission and was starting home."

Source:

https://www.familysearch.org/tree/person/memories/KWCT-N65

Volume 3 of the History of Andrew Jackson Stewart

Such a Rebuke

Benjamin Brown was a seeker, and after attending various churches and revivals, he went out of curiosity to a Latter-day Saint meeting, where he saw manifested the promised gifts of the Spirit. Having seen similar gifts elsewhere, he wasn't overly impressed or convinced. In fact, when he was invited to be baptized, he became very flippant and disrespectful. He started to read the Book of Mormon, but with an intent to prove it wrong. After reading ten pages, he rejected it altogether. He similarly felt inclined to reject his Bible. It was at this point that Benjamin realized something was very wrong. The spirit moving him was darkness— not light. He said:

> "The light that was in me became darkness, and how great it was, no language can describe. All knowledge of religious truth seemed to forsake me, and if I attempted to quote scripture, my recollection failed, after the first word or so!"

Recognizing what had happened to him, Benjamin determined to repent and start over with the Bible and then the Book of Mormon. Speaking of the Book of Mormon, he said:

> "I resolved to read it through, and I persevered in its perusal, till I came to that part where Jesus, on visiting the continent of America after his resurrection, grants the request of three of the apostles whom he had chosen to permit

them to live until His Second Coming on the earth."

At this point, Benjamin began to consider that the book might actually be true. He began to plead with the Lord to know if it was true, asking the Lord to let him, "see them (the Three Nephites) for a witness and testimony of the truth of the Book of Mormon, and I covenanted with him, if he complied with my request, that I would preach it, even at the expense of my life, should it be necessary."

As to what happened, Benjamin records:

> "The Lord heard my prayer, and about five days afterwards, two of the three visited me in my bedroom....One spoke to me for some time, and reproved me sharply on account of my behavior at the time when I first attended the meeting of the Saints and treated so lightly the gift of tongues. He told me never to do so again, for I had grieved the Spirit of the Lord, by whose power that gift was given. This personage spoke in the Nephite language, but I understood, by the Spirit which accompanied him, every word as plainly as if he had spoken in English...Such a rebuke, with such power, I never had in my life before or since, and never wish to have again. I was dumb before my rebuker, for I knew what he said was right, and I deserving of it."

At the conclusion of the interview, Benjamin described:

> "How these men went, I do not know, but directly they were gone. The Spirit of the Lord said to me, 'Now, you know for yourself! You

have seen and heard! If you now fall away, there is no forgiveness for you.'"

What was Benjamin Brown's response to such a manifestation? He said, "Did I not know then, that the Book of Mormon was true, and that Joseph Smith was a Prophet of the Lord? Surely, I did, and I do now, as surely as I know that I live."

Accordingly, Benjamin Brown was baptized in 1835, and would live out his days serving the Lord as a faithful priesthood man, missionary, and colonizer. He died in Salt Lake City, Utah on May 22, 1878. He was 83 years-old.

Source:

https://books.google.com/books?id=WjMEAAAAQAAJ&pg=PA36
&lpg=PA36&dq=%22as+I+found+it+stated+that+the+three+N
*ephites+had+power+to+show+themselves%22&source=bl&ots=z_*
KqorN1mZ&sig=bfPtpcyckwL-dFzaUD1Rk2bxadM&hl=en&sa=X&
ved=0ahUKEwje7Oa__YjaAhURy2MKHYBMCWEQ6AEIMDAC%
23v=onepage&q&f=false#v=onepage&q=%22as%20I%20found%20
it%20stated%20that%20the%20three%20Nephites%20had%20
power%20to%20show%20themselves%22 &f=false

https://www.familysearch.org/tree/person/memories/KWJP-QTH

Chapter Twenty-Eight

Such Is the Circle of Life

It was the Thanksgiving holiday in 2006. Pam and her husband Bill were visiting family in Utah. After dinner on one of those nights, a granddaughter announced, "Mommy is going to have a baby." When Pam turned to offer congratulations, she found her daughter-in-law, Necia, in tears. In her efforts to comfort her, she learned the following:

> "She had had a dream numerous times and… in her dream, she was pregnant. She received a phone call to tell her that Bill had died while driving a white SUV, and was T-boned by a semi. Her husband, my son, was also Bill. Her second child, a son, was William the fourth. So, to calm her, I told her there was NO WAY we were going to let my son drive a white SUV. Period. They had a maroon van and a blue Ford Expedition, so all seemed safe. I assured her that I would not let him drive my white Suburban which we had driven to Utah."

After the holidays, Pam and Bill returned home to New Mexico. Her daughter and her fiancée also came to visit for the Christmas holidays. It was on December 27th, that Pam was working when she got a call from the father of her daughter's fiancée, telling her that there had been a terrible accident near Farmington, Utah. Pam said:

"I rushed home as soon as I could and got a message on the phone to call the Farmington Hospital. A doctor came on the line and apologized. 'I'm sorry, but the only thing I can do is tell you that your husband and daughter have been killed in an auto accident with a semi-trailer. The young man with them has minor injuries and will be released in about an hour.' It was a 2 hour drive to Farmington from our home and a huge snow storm was moving in...so, I contacted my son who lived in the area and had him go rescue Cort, her fiancée. It turns out my husband had missed the sign for Chaco Canyon, tried to make a u-turn on a slightly curved hill, and in my white Suburban, was t-boned by a semi... When I had left for work early that morning, everyone was asleep, so I had no idea that they had made these plans. When I called my daughter-in -aw with the news, she screamed and dropped the phone. Her dream had come true, but not with her Bill, but with mine. She wanted to know why she was given this vision if there was nothing she could do to stop it. My answer, I believed, was to prove to me that this was meant to be."

A further witness to Pam that this was meant to be came when she learned that the first two people on the scene of the accident were a doctor and nurse on their way home from a shift at the hospital. A life-flight helicopter heard the 911 call and landed at the scene two minutes after the accident. Moreover, the doctor in the emergency room was the head of the New Mexico Trauma Surgeons' Association and the nurse with him was the head nurse of the hospital. In Pam's mind, there was comfort in knowing this was meant to be. Some days after the

tragedy, Pam's oldest son read the Patriarchal Blessing of Sarah, the daughter who had been killed. Pam said, "He came in and asked why no one had ever seen this phrase in her blessing: 'You are called to be a Missionary from Heaven, and for Heaven.' She was 21 at the time of her death."

About three months later, Necia was driving through Provo Canyon with two of her children when she hit black ice and lost control. When the vehicle came to rest, it was off the road in a field and on its wheels. The two children in the back seat were unscathed and their mother had a cut on her head. They were alright.

When the ambulance arrived, the EMT's commented about how lucky they were, considering the car must have rolled. The top was smashed in and all the windows were broken, but the 2 children didn't have a scratch on them. She then argued, saying that they hadn't rolled. She thought she had been awake, and was sure they didn't roll… As my daughter-in-law continued to argue with the EMTs, my two-year old grandson said something to the effect that "Grandpa pushed the car back up."

Years later, Pam's granddaughter, who was one of the children in that car, confided to her mother that she too remembered that day. She remembered that after the vehicle had stopped rolling, Sarah, the daughter who had been killed, was sitting in the front seat next to Necia, calling her by name, stroking her cheek and saying, "Wake up, you need to wake up." Pam concluded:

> "A dear friend of mine commented that if I had not lost my husband and daughter, I might have lost my grandchildren. Apparently, my daughter

had protected the kids from flying glass. Such is the Circle of Life and our help from the other side of the veil."

Source:

Pam Wade Family Records

Chapter Twenty-Nine

The Strength and Fierceness of a Tiger

Arza Adams shared common ancestry with the Prophet Joseph Smith, through John Lathrop, the minister, and through John and Elizabeth Howland of the Mayflower. He joined The Church of Jesus Christ of Latter-day Saints in Canada in December 1835, through the missionary efforts of John E. Page.

In 1838-39, Arza was among the saints in Missouri during the Mormon\Missouri War. During this difficult time, it is written in family records of him:

> "Arza Adams had the strength and fierceness of a tiger when molested. When trouble came, he met it halfway and more. He was in the hottest of the Missouri skirmishes. At one time, it is related he and fifteen companions, mostly boys, were being pursued by a mob of about two hundred. They were fleeing from their pursuers when Arza, angered by such treatment, urged the little group to make a stand and fight it out. They entrenched themselves on a wooded hillside and awaited the assault which never came. When the mob came close enough to see them, they made a hasty retreat. The group of boys were astonished. They could not understand why a mob which exceeded their number by more than one hundred should not attack."

A few years later, during the exodus of the Saints to the Rocky Mountains, Arza met one of the leaders of the mob that day.

> "He asked him why he and his followers had not made their planned attack. The mob leader said, 'There were hundreds of armed Mormons on that hillside. We knew we were running into a trap. We had to run for our lives.' Arza told him there were only fifteen young men with him on the hillside. But in the years that followed, he was never successful in convincing the mob leader that he spoke the truth. He insisted that he saw hundreds of armed men among the trees."

Arza was among those who entered into a sacred covenant to not rest until all the saints were delivered out of Missouri in 1839.

In June 1844, it was Arza who carried a letter from Carthage to Nauvoo, written by Elder John Taylor, who had been wounded at Carthage Jail.

Arza came to the Salt Lake Valley. In the summer of 1850, he went with others to do some trading in Provo. They camped near American Fork Creek and became impressed with the area. They returned to President Brigham Young and asked permission to settle the area.

President Young replied, "Go and take up what land you want." Heber C. Kimball, being present at the time, said, "At the time you are surveying your tract of land, I should like you to survey for me a tract adjoining yours."

The land was surveyed and Arza and others went back to lay claim to the land and prepare to bring in their cattle.

Arza's history says:

> "One day, while resting after dinner, I said, 'I am going to build me a house!' 'I am too,' said Washburn. The first two houses of American Fork were built. Cottonwood logs were used, and it was a difficult task. The trees were crooked, but after considerable trimming and patching, the houses were completed."

Arza would build, live, and serve the rest of his days in American Fork. He died on April 15, 1889, and was buried in American Fork Cemetery.

Source:
https://www.familysearch.org/tree/person/memories/KWJ6-SRZ

There Is No Mortal Way

Many of our ancestors who have left this life are anxious to share in the blessings of the temple. President M. Russell Ballard's grandfather, Henry Ballard, had a sacred experience while he was serving as the Bishop of the Logan Second Ward.

In 1884, the temple in Logan, Utah was almost ready to be dedicated. Henry Ballard had been involved in the building of this temple. He had a great desire to do work for his kindred who had passed on, and prayed that there would be some way that he could obtain the names of ancestors who had lived in England. The Logan Utah Temple was dedicated on May 17, 1884.

The next day, Bishop Ballard's daughters were playing outside of their home. Two men who they did not recognize approached them. One of the men gave the oldest daughter a folded newspaper and said, "Give this to your father and to no one else. Go quickly and don't lose it."

Bishop Ballard was busy interviewing members and writing temple recommends when his young daughter, Ellen, delivered a newspaper to him. The paper was the Newbury Weekly News, which was published in his birthplace of Newbury, Berkshire, England. The paper's date—May 15, 1884—indicated that it had been printed only three days earlier. At the time, a typical trip across the ocean, and then the plains, took weeks! Upon inspection, Bishop Ballard found the newspaper to contain a story with the names of sixty people who were buried in the Newberry cemetery and their accompanying dates of birth and death.

The next day, Bishop Ballard sought an explanation from Temple President Marriner W. Merrill. After listening to the bishop's story, President Merrill said, "Brother Ballard, someone on the other side is anxious for their work to be done and they knew that you would do it if this paper got into your hands." Bishop Ballard made certain the temple work was complete, and later it was learned that most of the people named in the newspaper were related to the Ballard family.

While serving as a missionary in England in 1950, a young M. Russell Ballard, the grandson of Henry Ballard, was serving a mission in England and made a visit to the offices of the Newbury Weekly News. "I visited the Newbury Weekly News," he records, "and verified that the newspaper had never been postdated or mailed out early. I held the issue of 15 May 1884 in my hands and photographed it. There is no mortal way that, in 1884, it could have reached Logan from Newbury within three days."

Source:
https://www.churchofjesuschrist.org/study/ensign/1987/07/missionary-journal?lang=eng

https://www.churchofjesuschrist.org/church/news/get-to-know-president-m-russell-ballard-inspired-teacher?lang=eng

This Is the Spirit of Understanding

Benjamin Brown was born September 30, 1794, in Queensbury, New York, the son of Asa and Sarah Moon Brown. Benjamin grew up a lad with little opportunity for education, but with a simple, trusting faith in the Lord and the Holy Bible. So pure was his childhood faith, that he said:

> "I can remember many times, on occasions of sickness among my relatives, while yet quite a boy, retiring to some barn or other convenient place of the kind, and there being suddenly restored to health in answer to prayers offered there, by me, on their behalf."

But then as the years passed, the boy came into contact with the sectarian churches of the day and their convoluted and conflicting interpretations of the scriptures, and before long, the Bible that had once been pure and simple, became, he said, "a perfect mystery." His simple faith was shaken and doubt and confusion took its place.

In time, Benjamin married and settled on a small farm of his own. More years passed, and then one day he came in from a hard day of work, and after eating supper, sat down by the fire. Suddenly, in the midst of his musings, a vision was opened to his mind. He saw his brother, who had died years before, in the act of earnest prayer. Benjamin "heard his voice clearly and distinctly and listened attentively." He heard his brother

speak of the great latter-day work to be done on the
earth before the Savior came, the gifts of the Spirit that
would be poured out, the great work of the gathering
of Israel, and other things that would make sense to
Benjamin only later. He heard his brother pray "for the
hastening of these things." Benjamin continued:

> "Soon he disappeared from my view, a sound,
> as of a rushing mighty wind, with some
> accompanying influence seemed to fill the house
> and myself and I heard a voice saying: 'This is the
> spirit of understanding.' An open Bible appeared
> before me, so peculiarly placed, that I could see
> portions of several books of the prophets and
> apostles at once." He said, "I began to read, [and]
> understanding and intelligence burst upon my
> mind, and the glory and beauty that seemed to
> shine forth…no language can describe."

His mind was opened. He saw and comprehended the
scriptures as he never had before. He was able to read
and understand whole chapters in the time it would take
to read a single verse. "With the rapidity of lightning"
doctrines of the Almighty were revealed to him along
with supporting passages from the writings of various
prophets and apostles on each subject. "I never before
saw such a connection between the scriptures." He knew
and comprehended:

> "That each and all of those men were inspired
> by the same Spirit and had a distinct knowledge
> of the same grand events and glorious truths,
> particularly those which I had heard my brother
> pray about." It was, he said, as though he saw
> "the whole at a glance, brought as it were to a
> focus."

Just then, his wife called out to him and the vision closed, but for some time after, he said, "The joy and peace with which my spirit was filled remained with me, and I glorified God."

The vision closed, but Benjamin knew, as he had never known before, the Spirit of understanding by which the scriptures were written, and are to be read, that the Holy Bible was true, and that the prophets and apostles of God were one in doctrine, principle, and power. Yet, it would be five more years before Benjamin Brown, the farmer, would be led to that church that embodied all the doctrine, gifts, and powers of the Holy Spirit his brother had prayed for.

Source:

https://books.google.com/books?id=WjMEAAAAQAAJ&pg=PA36
&lpg=PA36&dq=%22as+I+found+it+stated+that+the+three+N
*ephites+had+power+to+show+themselves%22&source=bl&ots=z_*
KqorN1mZ&sig=bfPtpcyckwL-dFzaUD1Rk2bxadM&hl=en&sa=X&
ved=0ahUKEwje7Oa__YjaAhURy2MKHYBMCWEQ6AEIMDAC%
23v=onepage&q&f=false#v=onepage&q=%22as%201%20found%20
it%20stated%20that%20the%20three%20 Nephites%20had%20
power%20to%20show%20 themselves%22 &f=false

https://www.familysearch.org/tree/person/memories/KWJP-QTH

What Is Your Trouble

It was about 1860 in Farmington, Utah. Lemuel Jerome Rice and other little boys went to watch the new piece of machinery operate. It was a threshing machine. Unfortunately, Lemuel happened to get too close to the machine and was pulled in. Before the men could stop the machine, "It seemed he was just pounded until there was hardly a bone that was not broken in his body." The workers were surprised when they pulled the boy from the machine and discovered he was still alive. "Everyone said, he couldn't possibly live." However, his mother just couldn't give him up. She had already lost three children and could not bear the thought of losing a fourth.

She asked the men to administer to him and they responded that it was of no use. "He couldn't possibly live." The men left to get others to assist in burying the boy. As soon as they were gone, Lemuel's mother, Elizabeth Elmira Rice, turned and saw a man with a white beard and white hair standing at her side. He said to her, "What is your trouble?" and she said she wanted someone to administer to him.

Evidently, the white-haired stranger agreed and laid his hands on the boy and proceeded to bless him by the authority of the Holy Priesthood. He promised that the boy would live. The family record states:

> "Little Lemuel started to revive, but when she turned to thank the man, he was gone, and she didn't see him leave. When her husband

and the men came to prepare him for burial…, they were surprised to see that he was alive. He completely recovered except that he had a slight limp all the rest of his life, but he recovered and grew to manhood and raised a big family."

May I say, again one more time, heaven is close and watching.

Source:
Loretta Rice Child Rice Interview by Nona M. Nebeker, August 20, 1972, in family biography, p. 4-5. Obtained from Beverly Watkins, Syracuse, Utah. January 2022.

33
Chapter Thirty-Three

Brigham and Joseph

On February 17, 1847, at a place called Winter Quarters, Nebraska, it would have been difficult to find a more burdened man for hundreds of miles than forty-six-year-old Brigham Young. His people were in exile. More than twelve thousand of them were scattered over ten thousand square miles, living in huts, tents, and even wagon boxes. They were looking to him for leadership, food, shelter, and a permanent home.

As the President of the Quorum of the Twelve Apostles, it fell to Brigham Young to lead the church following the death of Joseph Smith. It was a responsibility he neither asked for nor sought, but once called, he exercised untiring determination and cheer.

In the winter of 1847, hundreds of his people had died. Enemies from within and without challenged his right to lead and opposed him at every turn. When it was all over, history would remember Brigham Young as the man who finished what Joseph Smith started. But now, Brigham Young's greatness was yet to be realized.

At about noon on Wednesday, February 17, 1847, Brother Brigham lay in his bed asleep and very sick. At that hour, he dreamed a dream that he later described as follows:

> "I dreamed that I went to Joseph. He looked perfectly natural, sitting with his feet on the lower round of his chair. I took hold of his right

hand and kissed him many times, and said to him: 'Why is it that we cannot be together as we used to be? You have been from us a long time, and we want your society and I do not like to be separated from you.' Joseph, rising from his chair and looking at me with his usual, earnest, and pleasing countenance replied, 'It is all right.'

I said, 'I do not like to be away from you.' Joseph said, 'It is all right; we cannot be together yet, we shall be by and by, but you will have to do without me a while, and then we shall be together again.'

I then discovered there was a handrail between us. Joseph stood by a window and to the southwest of him it was very light. I was in twilight and to the north of me it was very dark; I said, 'Brother Joseph, the brethren you know well, better than I do, you raised them up and brought the Priesthood to us. The brethren have a great anxiety to understand the law of adoption or sealing principles; and if you have a word of counsel for me, I would be glad to receive it.'

Joseph stepped toward me, and looking very earnestly, yet pleasantly said, 'Tell the people to be humble and faithful, and be sure to keep the Spirit of the Lord and it will lead them right. Be careful and not turn away the small voice; it will teach you what to do and where to go; it will yield the fruits of the kingdom. Tell the brethren to keep their hearts open to conviction, so that when the Holy Ghost comes to them, their hearts will be ready to receive it. They can tell the Spirit of the Lord from all other spirits; it will whisper peace and joy to their souls; it will take malice, hatred, strife and all evil from their hearts; and their whole desire will be to do good, bring forth righteousness, and build up the kingdom of God. Tell the brethren if they will follow the Spirit of the Lord they will go right. Be sure to tell the people to keep the Spirit of the Lord; and if they will, they will find themselves just as they were organized by our Father in Heaven before they came into the world. Our Father in Heaven organized the human family, but they are all disorganized and in great confusion.'"

It seems the Prophet Joseph's counsel still applies to our day—and that one of the most important things we can and should do with our time each day is to prepare ourselves to be worthy to receive the influence of the Holy Spirit.

Source:
Brigham Young's Vision of Joseph Smith, Manuscript History of Brigham Young. 1847. 56.

34
Chapter Thirty-Four

Brigham Young Appeared Before Him

Francis Clement Nickle, or Clem as he was called, grew up deeply religious. At the age of eighteen, he became the superintendent of the Sunday School and the leader of the weekly youth prayer meeting in his Protestant church. Under his leadership, both prospered. Then one night after the prayer meeting, the youth were gathered outside the church. Some of them began to sing a party song, "Skip to my Lou." The minister overheard and was deeply offended. Clem was called in and "raked over the coals." He was dismissed as superintendent of the Sunday School and the youth prayer meetings were discontinued. It was not over yet. One day, a group of boys were gathered listening to Clem play the harmonica. Suddenly, one of them jumped up and started dancing a jig. Someone saw this and Clem was called before the elders of the church and excommunicated because he had "played for a dance."

Many years later, two Mormon Elders came into the community where they lived. The family history says:

> "Clem had been brought up where the Mormons were considered more as a band of outlaws than as a church. The missionaries seemed so clean and fine, so in earnest, that he took them in and listened to their message, believing, no doubt, that he might enlighten them and rescue them from a belief in pernicious doctrines."

Later that night, when he returned home, his wife Nellie asked, "How was their preaching?" to which Clem responded. "I've never heard so much truth in all my life, but it sounded hard to take at the last, for they said they knew Joseph Smith was a Prophet of God."

Clem continued to study and listen. The message rang true, but he wasn't sure. One day, he said, "Nellie, I'm going to see mother. I know that she will be happy to know the truth is really on the earth." To this Nellie heartily agreed.

Clem made the journey and told his mother who was also devout and a seeker.

> "Mother", Clem said, "I've come to tell you something glorious and beautiful. I have found the true church of Jesus Christ; one that bears His name and teaches His doctrines. It even has the same organization that He had in His church."

"Where is it, son, tell me quickly," she said. But as the conversation went on and she heard the despised word, "Mormon," she broke down and cried bitterly. "Don't ever let the Mormons into your home again, Clem," she said.

Though her words shook Clem, he and Nellie continued to investigate the church for many years. Finally, in November 1914, they were baptized. Clem was filled with joy and power, but there was a lingering pain in his heart. How could it be that his mother, a woman so noble and righteous, could "see no good in the church." It bothered him and "he longed for

a testimony strong enough that he would have power to put the message over to her and convince her of its truthfulness." One night, he knelt before his bed and prayed:

> "For a testimony so firm and true that he could stand before any force and declare its truthfulness with convincing power. Suddenly, the room became light and Brigham Young appeared before him, telling him that he had in very deed accepted the true gospel of Jesus Christ and promising him that if he would be faithful he would soon receive the Priesthood and that not only would his mother accept the truth, but that he would be instrumental in bringing all his father's household into the church."

Hearing that, Clem went forward with renewed effort to teach his mother, but she would not accept it. Then one day, his mother became ill and lapsed into a coma. All knew she was on her deathbed, when "suddenly, she regained full consciousness and she raised up in bed and called all her nine living children to her bedside, saying she had something she wished to tell them. Then she said, "Clem, I'm going and I want you to make me one promise before I go."

With some trepidation, he answered. "Mother, I will promise you anything that is within the bounds of reason."

"Clem," she said, "promise me that you will go to the temple and do the work for your father and me, and that you will teach the gospel as you understand it to all your brothers and sisters."

Through his tears of mingled grief and joy, he answered fervently, "With all the power God will give me, Mother, dear, I will." They all loved her very dearly, for she was an ideal mother; but they could not help thinking that maybe she was not quite rational as she spoke those words, so her daughter Emma said, "Mother, you don't mean that you want us to be Mormons, do you?"

"Yes, I mean that. Now I know that Clem has accepted the truth. I have seen into the eternities. I cannot talk more now, for I must go. But, and she pointed to him, Clem can talk and he can teach you the way." With these words she lay back on her pillow and passed away to her rest, having not only fulfilled the promise that Clem had been given in vision, that she would accept the truth, but she also was permitted to bear testimony of it to her children.

Clem did the temple work for his mother and father as requested. And—his prayer was answered. He became so powerful a teacher and missionary that he brought many to the gospel, among whom were "all his brothers and sisters."

Source:

https://www.familysearch.org/photos/artifacts/1192026

35
Chapter Thirty-Five

Carry On

Eliza waited a long time before she married—not that she didn't have suitors—she did, but she waited for that man with whom she could share her soul. Finally, in her 30's, she found him and they were married, but only for a short time. The love of her life was tragically killed. Eliza was "prostrated with grief and besought the Lord with all the fervency of her soul to permit her to follow her husband to the grave immediately, and not leave her in such a dark and wicked world."

So set was her mind on the matter that she did not, and could not cease that prayer of her heart. Then, from beyond the veil, her husband appeared to her and "told her that she must not continue to supplicate the Lord in that way, for her petition was not in accordance with his design concerning her. He told her that his work upon earth was completed as far as the mortal tabernacle was concerned, but her work was not. The Lord desired her, and so did her husband, to live many years." She was admonished to "be of good courage and help to cheer, and lighten the burdens of others, and that she must turn her thoughts away from her own loneliness, and seek to console her people in their bereavement and sorrow."

To her everlasting credit, she did. She obediently got up off her knees and went to work. When her people crossed the plains to the Rocky Mountains, she was there, among the first companies. She wrote of fording rivers, surviving raging storms, witnessing buffalo

stampedes, and walking for endless dusty miles. When her people were sick and struggling, Eliza was there, constantly lifting, encouraging, and blessing her people. Once in these mountains, she traveled far and wide, up and down the territory, carrying their history— teaching, organizing, and strengthening her people. She became one of the most powerful leaders and influential women of 19th century frontier America.

Besides the strength and charisma of her very character, Eliza led her people by her pen. She gained renown as a poetess. Through such poems as "O My Father, she would teach and administer comfort and joy to her people across generations, and down to the present day. Who was she— the woman so overcome with grief in the summer of 1844 that she wanted only to die? Eliza R. Snow!

In this life, when we think we are done and have no more to give—it is a surety that we are not! Carry on!

Source:
Andrew M. Jenson, Latter-day Saints Biographical Encyclopedia, Vol. 1, p. 695.

36
Chapter Thirty-Six

Eli H. Pierce and Angels

On October 5, 1875, Eli Pierce was sitting in a railroad telegraph office, smoking an old Dutch pipe and reading a novel. Though a Latter-day Saint, he was not attending the semi-annual General Conference of the church because, as he said. "I did not care to be." Eli was not a church-goer. He smoked cigars. In fact, he bought them by the thousands. He gambled, swore, and drank. He had scarcely read a dozen chapters of scripture in his life and had never preached a public discourse. "Nature," Eli said of himself, "never endowed me with a super-abundance of religious sentiment or veneration." That would be an understatement, it seems.

All of that notwithstanding, one of Eli's friends was in the conference and heard Eli's name read from the pulpit. He was being called to serve as a missionary in the eastern United States. The man ran out and immediately sent a telegraph. Eli received that telegraph. His first thoughts were, "I marveled and wondered if the Church was not running short of missionary material."

What he did next is truly remarkable:

> "As soon as I had been informed of what had taken place, I threw the novel in the wastebasket, the pipe in a corner, and started up town to buy scriptures, and have never read a novel nor smoked a pipe from that hour. I

sent in my resignation...to take effect at once, in order that I might have time for study and preparation."

And then Eli records this:

"Remarkable as it may seem, and has since appeared to me, a thought of disregarding the call, or of refusing to comply with the requirement, never once entered my mind. The only question I asked—and I asked it a thousand times—was: How can I accomplish this mission? How can I, who am so shamefully ignorant and untaught in doctrine, do honor to God and justice to the souls of men, and merit the trust reposed in me by the Priesthood?"

Determined to serve, Eli was mocked by some of his friends. They said he would not last six months. They were wrong. He arrived in Pennsylvania and went to work. At first, he did all he could to not speak in public, but in time, things changed. "Through prayerfulness, humility, and persevering faith, we soon obtained the coveted testimony," Eli wrote, "and were greatly blessed of the Lord in freedom of speech and delivery, and we became known in that locality as 'the boy evangelists.'"

It was on the mission that Elder Pierce had the following experience. He was called upon to bless the youngest child of the branch president. The mother, however, was embittered and refused to allow the dying child to receive the blessing. "Not wishing to intrude," Eli and the branch President retired to an upper room in the house to pray for the baby's life. The angry, suspicious mother sent one of her older daughters to

watch them. Elder Piece reported what happened:

> "In a secluded chamber, we knelt down and
> prayed earnestly and fervently until we felt that
> the child would live and knew that our prayers
> had been heard."

Then, turning around, they saw the girl standing in the
doorway, staring fixedly, but not at them. She seemed
focused on a certain point in the room. She said nothing,
until her father spoke to her, and then she said:

> "'Papa, who was that other man in there? He
> answered, 'That is Brother Pierce. You know him.'
> She said, 'No, I mean that other man.' 'There
> was no other, darling, except Brother Pierce and
> myself. We were praying for Baby.' She shook her
> head and said with perfect composure, 'Oh yes,
> there was. I saw him standing between you and
> Mr. Pierce and he was all dressed in white.'"

Elder Pierce concluded, "The baby was speedily restored
to perfect health."

In the period of his service, this unlikely servant of the
Lord baptized 108 people, blessed 37 children, organized
5 branches, held 249 meetings and traveled 9,870 miles.
His mission cost $1,320.

"And now," he concludes, "after years have passed, I
repeat, in words of soberness and in all sincerity, that the
happiest period of my life, as well as the most profitable,
was spent in the Master's service."

Source:

Biography and Family Record of Lorenzo Snow, pp. 407–13.

https://www.deseret.com/2010/12/15/20384744/an-unlikely-missionary-s-experiences

Elizabeth Crook Panting Cranney

Elizabeth Crook was born the second of eleven children, on October 7, 1827. She was baptized a Latter-day Saint by Wilford Woodruff on August 30, 1840. In 1848, she married Frederick Panting and they started a family. It was not a pleasant family life for Elizabeth. A number of children were born to the couple, but the thread of life was fine, and by 1856 all but two of her children had died. Her husband became a drunkard and cruel. He wanted nothing to do with the Mormons and demanded the same of her. To stop her from attending meetings, he would hide her shoes.

Elizabeth stubbornly refused to give in. She borrowed shoes from a neighbor and attended her meetings. Finally, her husband threatened that if she did not stop her association with the Mormons, he would kill her. Elizabeth took her two small children and fled. Elder Woodruff gave her a blessing that she would arrive safely. With faith in that blessing and nothing to sustain her, Elizabeth boarded the train, with her children, bound for Liverpool and her passage to America. Frederick Panting followed her and actually boarded her train. Strangely, he walked past her three times and failed to recognize her.

Elizabeth reached America and joined up with the Willie Handcart Company of 1856. She and her children partook of all the suffering and misery that came with that journey. At one point, Elizabeth's

daughter Jane became so ill that she lay in the handcart. Elizabeth could not stop to attend to her, but was forced to pull the handcart and keep moving, trusting her daughter to God.

With food supplies dwindling and members of the party dying daily, they stopped for camp one day. Elizabeth set out to gather buffalo chips to make a fire. A man came up to her and asked how the members of the company were. She told him that most of them were starving. He asked her to follow him and maybe he could help a little. She went with him. They went over a small hill out of sight of the camp. On the side of the hill was a cave. He led her into the cave. On one side of the cave was buffalo meat hanging up. The man loaded as much meat in her apron as she could carry and told her to share it with the other people. He then led her out the cave to the top of a small hill, pointed out the camp below, and told her not to get lost. As she turned back to thank him, he had disappeared. She looked for the cave and could find no trace of it.

She went back to camp and divided the meat with the ones most in need. It saved many lives.
Elizabeth and her children indeed reached Zion safely, where she remarried, kept the faith, and raised a large posterity.

Today, I went to church, and as I was leaving, a very elderly and frail sister whom I had never met, came up to me on the arm of her daughter. We shook hands. I was instantly caught by her eyes. Notwithstanding her age, they sparkled with light and intensity. The first thing she said to me was, "I am a great great granddaughter of Elizabeth Crook Panting Cranney."

And then she told me this story. My friends, this is why we endure in stubborn faith to the end—our lives of obedience and sacrifice now may be the very power that sustains our children and grandchildren later.

Source:
Great Great Granddaughter of Elizabeth Crook Panting Cranney

38
Chapter Thirty-Eight
Elizabeth Horrocks Jackson Kingsford

When Paul and Mormon discussed charity, the first
thing both of them said to describe it is charity
"suffereth long." Righteousness is not in how long we
suffer or who causes it, but how we endure it. Charity
suffereth long and is kind—not bitter. May I illustrate?

Aaron and Elizabeth Jackson and their three children
left for Zion in 1856. They soon found themselves
on the windswept plains of Wyoming, as part of the
Martin Handcart Company. Aaron came down with the
mountain fever and each day grew weaker and weaker.
On October 19th, at the last crossing of the North
Platte, Aaron started across, but the icy water was too
much. He sank down on a sandbar exhausted. He was
helped to his feet and a man on horseback carried him
across. No sooner were they on the bank when a terrible
storm of snow, hail, sand, and fierce winds struck.
Aaron was loaded into an empty cart and with his feet
dangling over the back panel and was carried to camp.
Elizabeth tried to feed him, but he had not the strength
to swallow. She put him to bed. The night was bitterly
cold. Sometime after midnight, Elizabeth awoke and
reached out for her husband. "I put my hand upon his
body, when to my horror I discovered that my worst
fears were confirmed. My husband was dead....The
elements had sealed up his mortal frame."

The next morning, while Elizabeth and her children
wept, the men of the camp covered Aaron and 13 others
in a grave of snow. "I will not attempt," Elizabeth
wrote, "to describe my feelings at finding myself thus

left a widow with three children, under such excruciating circumstances. I cannot do it. But I believe the Recording Angel has inscribed in the archives above, and that my sufferings for the Gospel's sake will be sanctified unto me for my good."

A few days later, the men of the camp were so weak that there was not one with strength sufficient to raise the tents. Elizabeth sat down on a rock, and with a child on her lap and one on each side, passed the night with nothing but the vault of heaven for a roof and the stars for companions.

Understandably, Elizabeth became despondent. "I was six or seven thousand miles from my native land, in a wild, rocky, mountain country in a destitute condition…and I, with three fatherless children, and scarcely nothing to protect them from the merciless storms."

That night, when Elizabeth went to bed, Aaron came to her and said, "Cheer up, Elizabeth, deliverance is at hand." The rescuers from the Valley had found them and took them to a place out of the worst of the elements called Martin's Cove. "The sufferings of the people were fearful," Elizabeth wrote, "and nothing but the power of a merciful God kept them from perishing."
Elizabeth and all three of her children made it to the Valley. To her posterity, down to the last generation, she wrote this:

> "I…desire them to know that it was in obedience to the commandments of the true and living God, and with the assurance of an eternal reward—an exaltation to eternal life in his kingdom, that we suffered these things. I hope, too, that it will inspire my posterity with fortitude to stand firm

and faithful to the truth and be willing to suffer, and sacrifice all things they may be required to pass through for the Kingdom of God's sake."

For her faith, Elizabeth was given the highest blessings that can be conferred upon any woman in mortality.

Source:
https://www.geni.com/people/
ElizabethKingsford/6000000018249545515

Ezra Thayer and The Book of Mormon

One morning, in the fall of 1825, an old gentleman went on his way through the New York countryside, singing joyfully. As he approached the door of a farmhouse, the owner, Ezra Thayer, opened the door. "Good morning, sir," said the old stranger. Ezra returned the greeting. "Do you ever give a stranger and a poor traveler something to eat?" he asked. Ezra replied, "Always."

Ezra described that he had never heard the hymn the old man was singing, but it seemed to "lighten up my soul," he said, "and filled it with the Spirit of the Lord." While his wife prepared breakfast, the old man asked Ezra questions which Ezra could not answer. The old man would smile and continue singing. Ezra said:

> "After eating, he put his chair back and continued with his singing for a little [while]. Then he arose and left the choicest blessings for me and my house and bid me goodbye. He stepped on the doorstep and as he let down the latch, I lifted it. As I opened the door, there was no man there. He could not possibly have gone out of my way, for I could see 40 or 50 rods all around. I searched every place for him. I called my wife out and we were astonished above all measure. I made mention of it 8 or 10 miles from home, and they said there had been just such a man who had been heard of in different places."

As time passed, other unusual and extraordinary manifestations were given to Ezra. Then, in the fall of 1830, he began hearing rumors about Joseph Smith and a new book he had translated called "The Book of Mormon". Thayer considered the story blasphemous and "was filled with wrath about it."

Ezra Thayer had known the Smith family. They had worked for him, and the idea that the uneducated Joseph Smith Jr. had the capacity to translate and publish a book of scripture was preposterous and impossible.

When some of his family showed an interest in learning more about the Book of Mormon, Thayer was angry. When some family members took his horses and went to hear Hyrum Smith preach, Thayer scolded them and demanded that they "not take his horses again to hear those blasphemous wretches preach." In fact, he was angry enough that he offered to loan "a pair of horses to take Joseph Smith to prison."

Though his family insisted there was something to the message and that he ought to give it a chance, he remained aloof and angry. Finally, his brother came and asked him to go and hear the preaching. After all, what harm could come in just listening. Reluctantly, Ezra agreed to go.

It was Sunday, October 5, 1830 when the two brothers rode up to the Smith Family log cabin in Palmyra Township. There was a large, spreading crowd gathered around to hear Hyrum preach. Ezra "rushed in and got close to the stand, so as to be particular to hear what was said." He said:

"When Hyrum began to preach, every word touched me to the inmost soul. I thought every word was pointed to me...I could not help myself. The tears rolled down my cheeks. I was very proud and stubborn. There were many there who knew me...When Hyrum got through, he picked up a book and said, 'Here is the Book of Mormon.' I said, 'Let me see it.' I then opened the book, and I received a shock with such exquisite joy that no pen can write and no tongue can express. I shut the book and said, 'What is the price of it?' "Fourteen shillings,' was the reply. I said, 'I'll take the book.' I opened it again, and I felt a double portion of the Spirit. That I did not know whether I was in the world or not, I felt as though I was truly in heaven."

As Ezra and his brother started for home, his brother asked what he thought of The Book of Mormon, Ezra answered "It is true as sure as God sits upon his throne."

Soon thereafter, Ezra Thayer was baptized and called on a mission. At his request, the Lord gave a revelation to Ezra Thayer. Three times he was commanded to open his mouth and the Almighty would fill it. Ezra was faithful and immediately set out preaching the Gospel. As he declared it, "When God shows a man such a thing by the power of the Holy Ghost, he knows it is true. He cannot doubt it"–and of the Book of Mormon, Ezra never did. There is a power in the Book of Mormon that is off the grid for mortals to comprehend.

Source:

http://www.sidneyrigdon.com/dbroadhu/OH/sain1860.htm

https://www.churchofjesuschrist.org/study/manual/revelations-in-context/ezra-thayer-from-skeptic-to-believer?lang=eng

https://www.josephsmithpapers.org/person/ezra-thayer

40
Chapter Forty

Family Visit

Pernilla Nilsdotter Bom Nielson was a faithful Swedish church member who, at the age of 45, immigrated to Utah in 1863. She was assigned to the John F. Sanders Company, along with her three youngest children, one who died on the pioneer trail. Because of limited funds, her husband and teenage son made the journey two years later. The family settled in Fairview, Sanpete County, Utah. Though their material possessions were meager, they were happy to be among the church members in Utah and enjoy the blessings of the gospel. Pernilla helped in the home and did work for other people to help support herself and her family. She was faithful and helped others with her skills of sewing, cooking, candle making, spinning wool, and weaving cloth. She often bore her testimony of the truths of the Restored Gospel.

Pernilla had known much sorrow because of the death of close family members who were dear to her. She was the oldest and only surviving child of Karna Jönsdotter and Nils Bom. Nine of her brothers and sisters died in infancy, and the family coped with their seemingly endless grief by memorizing large sections of the Bible. Her dear parents died within days of each other in 1855.

During her marriage to Ole, they had nine children. Only four grew to adulthood. She buried two infants, a two-year-old boy, two four-year-old girls, and a seven-year-old boy. Her son, Pehr, drowned at the age of 20 on the Green River, during a mission to bring immigrants to Utah. Finally, her husband Ole died after a long illness at the age of 55. Thoughts of beloved family members in the Spirit World were constantly a part of her.

Late in Pernilla's life, she was at her home in Fairview, Utah. Her sons, Lars and Swen, were adults and living on their own. Her youngest son, Ole Jr., now a young man, was watching over his mother and taking care of her home and property. One evening, while he was cutting wood, he saw a group of people enter his mother's home. He gathered up the wood and went to the house to see who the guests were. To his surprise, when he entered there was no one there but his mother. He asked her if she had visitors. She said, "There were some people here from our departed family who asked me to do their temple work." With so many ties to loved ones in the Spirit World, it is not surprising that they would reach out to her for help.

Pernilla did the work for many of her relatives in the Manti Temple before she passed away on December 20, 1898 in Fairview, Utah.

Source:
https://www.familysearch.org/tree/person/memories/KWJF-LPV

Family history records and "Pioneer Women of Faith and Fortitude Volume 3. International Society Daughters of the Utah Pioneers, 1998, page 2176.

Feramorz Young

Feramorz Little Young was an exceptional young man. He was born September 16, 1856 in Salt Lake City to Brigham and Lucy Decker Young. He was the sixth of seven children and grew up in the Beehive House. He attended school at the University of Deseret and then at age 16, he entered the United States Naval Academy. By age 21, he had graduated from the Troy Polytechnic Institute. As a student, he excelled.

As a Latter-day Saint ,he was a stripling son of courage, defending the faith constantly during his time in the east. Then, in November 16, 1880, Fera Young left Salt Lake City to serve as a missionary in Mexico City. His diary is filled with those entries typical of any young man serving as a missionary.

Towards the end of his mission, he began to feel unwell. Along with Elder Moses Thatcher, Elder Young began his journey home. While at sea, Fera grew worse and began to sense that he was not going to live. Finally, on September 27, 1881, just off the coast of Havana, Cuba, Elder Feramorz Young passed away and was buried at sea.

His passing was a great trial to Elder Thatcher, and also to his family and friends. How could such a pure and intelligent young man, capable of doing so much good, be called home? What a terrible loss. His mother would say of him that she "could not remember a word, thought, or act of his life that would bring her the least

sorrow or uneasiness." Fera's closest boyhood friend would later say of him, "If ever there was a clean, sweet, absolutely pure young man upon the earth, he was that young man."

In most instances, the story, tragically, ends there–but not this time.

Years later, a woman who not a Latter-day Saint, but a stranger, came to the home of Lucy Decker Young, Fera's mother and related the following story:

> "Now Mrs. Young, I do not believe a thing of what I am going to tell you. This girl friend of mine was one of the noblest, finest, choicest kind of girls and young women that ever lived. She has come to me in this city of Salt Lake on three separate occasions at night in dreams, and has given me this information: the date of her birth, the date of her death, and all that is necessary, she says, for a record in the Temple: and she has told me that your son, Feramorz L. Young has converted her and that in addition to converting her he has proposed marriage to her."

The young woman then commanded her doubting friend to go to Sister Young and tell her the story and vouch for her virtue and integrity. This young woman had not grown up in Salt Lake City, and this woman was the only one who knew her and could vouch for the uprightness of her life. The young woman requested that her work be done and that she be married by proxy to Fera.

The woman said again to Mother Young, "I do not believe a word of it," but then she seemed to plead for

Sister Young to do something because she said, "the last time this young woman came to me she said, 'You might just as well go to Mrs. Young and give her this information, because I am going to come and come and come until you do it'"

The woman then said, "I just cannot bear to have her come again."

"This beautiful girl was sealed to Brother Young, and I am convinced that my dear friend lost nothing by dying in his youth." So said President Heber J. Grant in February 1931.

Source:

https://archive.org/stream/improvementera3404unse#page/n6/mode/1up

https://lib.byu.edu/collections/mormon-missionary-diaries/about/diarists/feramorz-little-young/

Go to the Place of Gathering

In September 1830, twenty-year-old Chapman Duncan left his home in Barnet, New Hampshire, bound for South America. He was suffering from what was called consumption and determined to go south for his health. The route he chose to get there was to travel to Cincinnati, Ohio and from there, south down the river systems to New Orleans.

While journeying on the Ohio Canal, he became so ill that he was confined to his bed. Somewhere near Louisville, Kentucky, he was lying awake in his bed when he had the following experience:

> "It appeared as though a man spoke, yet I heard no audible voice; it was a quiet, peaceful, yet sure impression. In fact, I knew that the Lord or an angel spoke to me. This is the message he bore to me: 'Thou shalt prosecute thy journey no farther south than the mouth of the Ohio river. If you do, you shall die.' I looked to see the personage. I saw none. I began to meditate upon what I had heard and the feeling that pervaded my person, and while thinking, I cannot say whether it was five minutes or more, the Spirit again spake and said further, 'If thou wilt go to the place of gathering of my people, thou shalt live.' The force of the message rested so heavily upon me that I dare not go farther south and turned my course for St. Louis, Missouri."

Chapman became discouraged when he could see no way he could get to St. Louis. He called on the Lord in prayer. Shortly after, he saw two men standing on the wharf. He felt impressed to go talk to them. One of the men was Elder Philo Dibble, a member of The Church of Jesus Christ of Latter-day Saints. Chapman later recalled, "My soul was filled with joy to think the Lord would make plain the way for me to do his commandments and place means within my reach as he did there."

Chapman set out for Independence, Missouri in November 1830, driving a wagon for Philo Dibble. He wrote of the warm welcome he received when he arrived:

> "After listening to the doctrine of Christ and getting somewhat acquainted with the new-made friends (for they took me in), I joined the Church, I think the last of December, baptized by Elder Titus Billings on the Sabbath day, confirmed by Bishop Partridge and council. In a short time, the Holy Ghost fell upon me and I did speak with new tongues and prophecy, and I thanked the name of my Redeemer."

From that point forward, Chapman Duncan cast his lot with the Saints. He lived to be 88 years-old and passed away in Caineville, Wayne County, Utah.

Source:
https://www.familysearch.org/tree/person/memories/KWJY-48Q

Gustavus Perry

The story is told, by the descendants of Gustavus and Eunice Perry, of a dark stormy night, probably early in the year 1830, in the region of Lewis, Essex County, New York. The work was done for the day on the farm, and the family was gathered in their kitchen. Their front door opened and a stranger entered the room. He was an old man with a long, flowing, white beard. The family noted that even though it was a stormy night, there were no signs of rain on him.
The old man blessed them in the name of the Lord and asked for food and lodging for the night, both of which were generously given. Somewhere in those first moments, he took a pack from his shoulder, opened it ,and pulled out a puppy which he gave to the children to play with.

Later that evening, he took from his pocket a book from which he began to read, "Telling them that…. [the book] was soon to come forth and telling them to get one at their first opportunity."

The next morning, he mysteriously disappeared. None of the neighbors saw him go, even though it was open daylight. Not long after, two elders from The Church of Jesus Christ of Latter-day Saints came into the area, preaching about The Book of Mormon.

"The family obtained one and in reading the book, they recognized passages of scripture the stranger had read to them on the night of his

 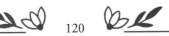

visit. In the year 1832, the family joined The Church of Jesus Christ of Latter-day Saints."

From that point forward, where the church went, the family of Gustavus and Eunice Perry was there. Eventually, they settled in what would be known as Perry, Utah. Their second great grandson was L. Tom Perry of the Quorum of the Twelve Apostles.

Source:
https://www.familysearch.org/tree/person/memories/LH23-P4R

44
Chapter Forty-Four
He Lifted the Car

The year was 1979. Lindy and her mom and sister were leaving the parking lot of the Bernina sewing store in downtown Logan, Utah. Because of construction, there was a very deep gutter running alongside the exit from the parking lot. Lindy's mom, who couldn't see very well, accidentally drove over the edge. The front of the car dropped two feet down into the gutter and was stuck fast. They tried to reverse out, but the car would not budge. Just then, a young man happened to drive by. He saw their situation, backed up, and jumped out. Lindy describes what happened next:

> "He then got down in the gutter in front of the car and instructed my mom to put the car in reverse. Then he told her to gun it and lifted the car. He had some major muscle power going on…. Somehow he lifted the car up with all of us in it, and put us back safely onto the parking lot. He then promptly left, without saying a word to anyone. I remember he had brown hair and glasses."

Now, just for the record, this was no smart car or golf cart. It was a massive 1979 Plymouth with a V8 engine, weighing in at about 3,858 pounds. We used to call these cars "lead sleds."

Lindy added the postscript that, "Not sure if this would be possible for a human, but it definitely happened. I was there."

Question: Was this an angel or a mere mortal? Answer: Does it matter? When we undertake to help those who can't help themselves, we are doing what angels do—we are angels! Could you be someone's angel today?

Source:
Contributed by Lindy Taylor

45
Chapter Forty-Five

He Put Me on My Knees

It was April 1878, just north of Grantsville, Utah. Young Orrin Orlando Barrus and his older brother were driving a large herd of cattle to fresh grazing. As the stock attempted to cross an alkali swamp, they became mired down. The swamp was about 100 yards across. The animals struggled against the mud, but could not extricate themselves, and the boys were powerless to help them. Finally, Orlando's brother took off for town to get help.

"I was left to stand guard over the herd and await his coming," Orlando said. "While performing this service, I became somewhat excited upon seeing several of our most valuable animals struggling and plunging in the swamp. They sunk deeper and deeper into the quicksand and mire until only the heads of some of them could be seen, the rest of their bodies having sunken out of sight."

Desperately, Orlando wondered what to do. It was at that moment that he remembered his mother teaching him that when he was in trouble and needed help, he should pray.

"I raised my hand and arm to the square," he said, "as I had seen our brethren do in opening a meeting, stood up and removed my hat, and earnestly implored my Heavenly Father to take our animals out of the predicament they had gotten themselves into. No sooner had I offered

 124

this prayer, than some power put me on my knees and a voice seemed to say, "Pray again". This I did more earnestly than before, if possible, asking the Lord to get the cows out of the mire as quickly as he possibly could. I had an assurance right there and then that it would be done."

At the conclusion of the prayer, Orlando ran to the top of a sand knoll and looked to see if his brother was coming. Not far away, he spied his brother and two of his uncles returning with a large span of horses and chains to drag the cattle free. Orlando continued:

"With them, I returned to the spot where the struggle was going on, when to the great astonishment of my brother and uncles, all of the aforesaid animals were completely out of the swamp. They were peacefully grazing on the green grass of the next sand knoll, and so covered with mud that they all seemed the same color (black)."

How did the animals get free? Orrin's uncles laughed and accused the boys of crying wolf, but it was evident that something extraordinary had happened, but what?

"I knew," he said, "but I was afraid to tell them how it happened, for fear they would doubt and would laugh, and would treat a sacred thing lightly. I knew that the Lord had answered my prayer and had taken the cattle out of the mire. Just how it was done, I did not know, but we saw someone leaving the swamp, as we came on the scene, riding a large horse or mule. He was only a hundred yards or so away, but he never came to receive our thanks or to tell what he had done, and I am convinced that no human could have

done such a big job in such a short time. We went over where he was seen and discovered the tracks of a large shod horse or mule in the sand."

Orlando concluded:

"I know as I know that I live, that God heard and answered the prayer of a little boy and that the best attitude for prayer is on the knees for he put me on my knees when I was standing up praying, and he said to me 'pray again.' Just how He did it, I do not know, but I believe the man on a horse was from another world."

Source:
https://www.familysearch.org/tree/person/memories/KWCH-CRD

Story contributed by Lindy Taylor

He Was Gone

David Cluff had a large family and lived in Nauvoo, Illinois. He was a prosperous carpenter and a farmer, but then he answered the call and served as a missionary in the eastern states.

Upon his honorable release, he returned to Nauvoo and his family with a desire to return to work in his cabinet shop. However, in his absence, his carpenter tools had worn out, and given the family's present poverty, getting new ones "seemed impossible."

He was faced with a dilemma. He needed new tools to do quality work, but he did not have the means to do that work to buy the new tools. He said to his wife, "Mother, I do wish I could get ahead enough to buy a set of tools."

His son, Benjamin, heard that comment. A few days later, Benjamin happened to be playing in the street in front of their home. He and the other boys witnessed "A strange-looking man with a small pack on his back, such as carpenters sometimes carry tools in as they go from job to job." Benjamin observed that he turned through the gate and walked into his father's shop.

Curious, Benjamin followed the man in and heard him say to his father, "Don't you want me to make you some tools?" "Yes," came the reply. "I am needing some tools very badly, but I don't know how I can pay you." The stranger responded, "Never mind about the pay. Have

you any seasoned lumber?" David Cluff pointed to some seasoned maple at the north end of the shop and the stranger went to work—for three weeks!

Benjamin said, "When this was done, he asked father if there was anything else he wished to have done. Father replied that he had fit him up in pretty good shape. Now, said father, "How can I pay you?" Then came the strangest part of the miracle, for when father asked the question, 'How can I pay you?' The stranger replied, "You can pay me the next time you see me."

The stranger then picked up his tools, bid David goodbye and walked out. Young Benjamin followed him out and stood at the gate, watching him walk away. He said:

> "Before the stranger had gone fifty yards from the gate, my attention momentarily was drawn off, but resuming my gaze after the stranger, I was exceedingly astonished. The road was open. There was no corner, no tree, shrubs or any other obstruction that he could secrete or hide himself behind, but he was gone from my view."

David Cluff took those tools and went to work building the Nauvoo Temple.

Source:
https://www.familysearch.org/photos/artifacts/91897002?p=2
9415216&returnLabel=David%20Cluff%20Sr.%20(KWJ6-
TK8)&returnUrl=https%3A%2F%2Fwww.familysearch.org%2Ftree
%2Fperson%2Fmemories%2FKWJ6-TK8

I Grabbed That Hand

Diana went to church with a friend and enjoyed the sermon that was offered. After it was over, she asked her friend if there was more. Her friend asked, "What do you mean?" and Diana said, "I don't know. My chest feels like there should be something more."

That night, she went home, deep in thought. Before crawling into bed, she knelt down and asked Heavenly Father if there was a church on the face of the earth that had all his truth in it? As she described it, she didn't want to bounce around from church to church, picking up truth here and there. That night, Diana experienced a dream:

"In my dream, I stood in a room that was divided down the middle by a line. I stood on the line and on the right side of me were people and noise and partying, and on the left side of me were white walls. I looked at the right side and said, " I'm going over to that side." Somewhere in my dream, a fire broke out and I could not get out of the room. There were no doors and no windows. I began to panic and thought I didn't want to die. I haven't done what I'm supposed to do. I looked to the left side of the line and all I saw was a hand, the cuff of a white shirt, and the cuff of a blue suit jacket. I grabbed that hand and I was pulled to the line, and I woke up. It was morning. I thought that was the strangest dream I have ever had in my whole life, and I had no idea what it meant."

Later that same evening, Diana went to visit her grandmother. While there, a knock came at the door. She opened it and there standing in front of her were two smiling, young men. One of them reached out his hand. Diana looked down. She said:

"All I saw was the hand, the cuff of a white shirt, and the cuff of the blue suit jacket. I took that hand, and he said, 'We are missionaries for The Church of Jesus Christ of Latter-day Saints and we have a message for you'. I teared up and said, "I know."

She invited them in. As they taught her about the Prophet Joseph Smith, her heart raced because it was all so familiar—like she had heard it before. She was baptized one month later and is faithful to this day.

Sometimes the angels and messengers of the Almighty are as mortal as we are.

Source:
Story contributed by Diana Paquette

Chapter Forty-Eight

I Suffered Worse Than a Thousand Deaths

The year was 1831. Twenty-seven-year-old Hervey Green heard about a new church called "Golden Bible Folks." His first reaction was, "What will people get up for religion next?"

Then he learned that members of that church, now called "Mormons," were going to be preaching in his area. He attended and said, "Ere I was aware of it, I was a believer." He returned home and began reading the Book of Mormon. At length, he determined to go to Kirtland and "see Joseph Smith for myself." He was baptized into the church on the way.

Upon his arrival he said:

> "I beheld a prophet of the Lord, and while gazing upon Joseph and Hyrum Smith, a strangely new sensation crept over me and I was in the presence of one who had seen a holy angel, and to whom God had spoken....I felt a child in his presence. Much like the disciples at the feet of the divine Master and great Father, I sat and eagerly fed upon the wonderful words of life that fell from his inspired lips."

Then Hervey makes this solemn declaration, "The glorious reality was mine, and I laid hold of it with a full determination never to let it slip from my possession, come weal or woe, come life or come death."

In early June, 1831, a conference was held on the Isaac Morley farm. It was at that conference that the first high priests of this dispensation were ordained. At the conference, Hervey records Joseph as saying:

"My brethren, this is a day of power in which God will manifest unto you some of the great operations of His Spirit in a degree which has not been known upon this land since the Nephites enjoyed it here; and the power of the adversary will also be made manifest to like manner; and by this you may learn the workings of the two powers, that you may be able to detect the workings of the adversary; for it shortly goes forth with lying wonders to the world, and will closely follow and imitate the power of God, and thus deceive many; for behold, the Spirit of God is here to work in power, and the spirits of darkness, even devils, are here also in much power."

As Joseph made that promise, the powers began to work among the brethren. Some saw angels, visions and the Savior himself, while others, like Hervey, were seized with a different power. He records:

"At the same time others, including Elder H. S. Whitlock and myself, were suddenly seized with an unseen power, and violently thrown to the floor. Some writhed in horrible convulsions, making efforts to preach and speak in tongues, imitating others. I was tightly bound and held in awful suffering and fearful suspense, so that I could not breathe nor move a finger to save me. I knew it was the power of the devil, and I could do nothing but think and suffer, horrified

at the thought of being wholly in his power. My thoughts flew like lightning, my anguish knew no bounds. In that brief time of some twenty minutes in this terrible agony, I suffered worse than a thousand deaths. Joseph, in tears, finally said, 'It is enough;' and then, in the true majesty of a prophet and servant of God he, in the name of Jesus Christ, rebuked the devils, commanding them to depart out of me, which they immediately did. And, oh! What a load like a heavy, killing weight rolled off and left me. Immediately, I commenced praying to God, calling upon Him for some time with much anxiety to preserve me from another such visitation of that terrible power of Satan. This occurrence fully convinced me of what I had before doubted, the existence of real devils here, in such power. My heart was drawn out in fervent prayer the entire night following, that the Lord would not again suffer me to be bound and overcome by the powers of darkness."

The next day was the Sabbath. Hervey lingered behind as everyone made their way to the conference. He wanted to be alone to pray. Suddenly, two glorious heavenly beings appeared to him that he did not identify. One vanished quickly, while the other extended a copy of The Book of Mormon towards him. He says:

"Immediately, all my fear of being bound again left me. The Holy Spirit rested upon me, and I was completely happy as I before had been completely miserable. The scriptures unfolded to my understanding, and it seemed that all things around me were new."

From that point forward, Hervey was dedicated. He served numerous missions and was even beaten by a mob, until he was near death, for his testimony. He saw miracles and wonders, but then, after the death of the Prophet Joseph Smith, Hervey would not accept the authority of Brigham Young and the Twelve. He went west, but soon apostatized and went to California where he joined another church. Thus it is that we know little of Hervey Green, notwithstanding his wonderful service.

No matter who we are or what we have seen, if we do not continue humbly seeking the Lord and His holy word—daily, we can fall!

Source:
From the autobiography of Hervey Green.

https://www.familysearch.org/tree/person/memories/KWJR-JBT

If You Are of the Lord,
I Will Be Healed

In the year 1805, Joseph Murdock was injured while lifting a heavy, green log. He was twenty-two years old. From that point on, he was crippled, unable to work, and never free of pain. Add to that, as the years passed, Joseph came down with consumption, which we know today as tuberculosis. Through the many years of illness, Joseph became a student of the Bible. He became convinced that none of the churches were the Lord's church. He also believed that the true gospel would be restored. By 1836, Joseph Murdock was so ill that it was feared he would not recover. His son, Joseph, records:

> "An Elder of The Church of Jesus Christ of Latter-day Saints, by the name of Jonathan Dunham, called at our home and appeared to be anxious to see my father. He went to father's side, and my father asked him if he really believed in the new religion. Elder Dunham replied that he did, with all his heart and soul, that it was the true religion restored through the Prophet Joseph Smith, the same gospel that was practiced by Jesus Christ. My father said to Elder Dunham, 'Either you have the true gospel or you are the greatest imposter in the work of the Lord,' Then he said, 'Now, if you have the truth and are of the Lord, I want you to pray for me, and lay your hands upon me, and if you are of the Lord I will be healed, and if you are an imposter, I will not be healed'. Elder Dunham

knelt down and prayed for father, got up and laid his hands on his head, blessed him, and asked the Lord to heal him of his long sickness and suffering."

The family records continue:

"Joseph wrote that his father fell into a deep, sound sleep, his face peaceful and serene, and for the first time in years untroubled by pain. In the morning, he awoke rested and refreshed and called for his clothes. Sally, at first refused to give them to him, but he told her, 'I am a well man, give me my clothes.' So she did as he asked and he dressed himself and for the first time in years walked to the table where he ate breakfast with his family. Sally had been ill for many years also and was often confined to her bed, although we don't know what her ailment was, but after Elder Dunham administered to her, she was made well in a day, and suffered no further afflictions for the rest of her days."

The entire family joined the church. Then, in 1842, Joseph Sr. suffered a stroke and was again crippled. It was at this time that the family began the journey to join the Saints in Nauvoo. It was a very difficult trip. By the time they arrived, he had become deaf and deranged and was unable to even stand up. His son, Joseph, was determined to get him to the Prophet Joseph Smith. He did so and left this record:

"Brother Joseph made him a promise in the name of Israel's God that if he would be baptized in the Mississippi River seven times, he should be made whole in one week. This was

complied with and he was made whole in the time set apart, never to be anymore afflicted in life."

Joseph Stacy Murdock gave this witness of his father's healing, "I bear testimony to what I have written as an eyewitness."

On Oct. 9, 1844, Joseph passed away. According to the family records:

> "His wife, Sally, never completely shared her husband's zeal for the church and after his death she took her eleven-year-old son, Nymphus, and boarded a river boat to begin the long trip back to her old home. But only one day's travel from Nauvoo, something happened that changed her entire life as well as the lives of all of her family. That night, Sally was visited by a vision of her husband, and Nymphus later testified that his father appeared before them. He asked Sally, 'Where are you going? You gave me your promise that you would see our son Nymphus raised in the church and go with its body to Zion!' At dawn's first light, Sally left the river boat and with Nymphus made her way back to Nauvoo."

She never left the church again. She took her family and went west, settling in Salt Lake City. It was written of her:

> "On Sept. 25, 1864 Sally Stacy Murdock died at the adobe brick home she and Nymphus had built at 3rd South and Main Street in Salt Lake City, Utah. She was 86 years of age.... She had suffered through the trials at Nauvoo and the hard times at Winter Quarters.... She was always the first to

help the less fortunate and was beloved by all. She was a stalwart in the Church and raised her sons to become the pioneers, colonizers and church leaders they became noted for."

Joseph and Sally Stacy Murdock—true and faithful!

Source:

https://www.familysearch.org/tree/person/memories/KWJD-VKH

Little James Nathaniel

On Wednesday, August 31, 1853, Israel Barlow stood in a small cemetery in the village of Nauvoo, Illinois. In his heart, he carried the request of his grieving wife that he find the grave of their firstborn son, James Nathaniel, who had lived but one day and died on May 8, 1841. Israel, a seventy, was on his way to England to preach the Gospel. As he had departed his family in Salt Lake, his wife asked him to stop and see their son's grave. Rumors had reached them that a road was being built over that Mormon cemetery, and would he move the body of their son to the cemetery east of town? Israel agreed to do so.

As he stood in the cemetery, he was unable to determine where the grave was located. Weeds and neglect had taken over the sacred place. Israel searched and could not find it. The next day, he enlisted the help of another man and together they found the grave of little James and his cousin side by side. The coffins were very much decayed and Israel decided that he would not move them. He turned and began to walk away, but then he stopped and looked back. Looking at the little coffin, something said to him "Move it. Move it!" But Israel was running short of time. He had to catch a boat and continue his journey and this looked like a lot of work. He turned away again thinking to himself, "The earth as well as the sea would have to give up its dead and…that they might as well be in one place as in another. I therefore turned away," he said, "and concluded that I would leave them there."

Israel had gone only a few feet when another voice came into his mind so clear and distinct that he could not argue with it, "Daddy, do not leave me here."

Israel turned back, and with a greater peace than he had yet known, he removed the body of his infant son to the old cemetery east of Nauvoo, conscious that he had done his duty by the Lord and his son. He carved a stone to mark the final resting place of James Nathaniel Barlow, and as he was about to leave something held him.

> "The time of my departure had come" he said. "Could I go away? No! There was something that caused my feelings to linger there and bound me fast. ...I felt a desire to dedicate myself and all that I might call mine own into the hands of the Lord that I might be counted worthy to come forth with [my son] in the morning of the First Resurrection. The thoughts of absenting myself far away never more in life to return to his grave wrung the last thread of affection I bore till it was broken with tears on his grave."

Israel Barlow went on into history, firm in the hope of the coming day when that grave would be opened one final time.

It was Joseph Fielding Smith who said, "It remains the responsibility of each individual to know his kindred dead....even if the [Temple] work is done, then it is still each person's responsibility to study and become acquainted with his ancestors" (Ensign July 2009, p. 35).

Source:

Ora H. Barlow, The Israel Barlow Story and Mormon Mores, (1968), 306-08

https://familysearch.org/photos/documents/5887790

Lydia Knight

Repeatedly, the Almighty has admonished us to "be strong and of a good courage; be not afraid." Most people neglect to connect the next thought that explains how this is to be done. It continues, "For the Lord thy God is with thee whithersoever thou goest" (Joshua 1:9).

Lydia Goldthwait was born in 1812, in Massachusetts. Hers was a happy childhood. When she was 16, she met and married a handsome and charming fellow, but when he turned to drinking, her marriage became "the story of a man's cruelty and a woman's suffering."

In 1829, Lydia gave birth to a little girl who proved to be a blessing of comfort to a youthful mother. Two years later, her husband abandoned her. Six months later, a little boy was born, but he lived only a short time. Then one year later, her little girl died also. Lydia was inconsolable.

Freeman Nickerson, a family friend, was moved to help the sorrowing girl. He invited her to come to Canada and live with him and his wife. While there, Lydia met Joseph Smith the Prophet and heard him preach. She saw "his face become white and a shining glow seemed to beam from every feature."

Lydia was converted and with "trembling joy" was baptized. Shortly after, as Joseph was preparing to leave, he paced back and forth in deep thought. Finally, he spoke:

"I have been pondering on Sister Lydia's lonely
condition, and wondering why it is that she has
passed through so much sorrow and affliction
and is thus separated from all her relatives. I now
understand it. The Lord has suffered it even as He
allowed Joseph of old to be afflicted, who was sold
by his brethren as a slave into a far country, and
through that became a savior to his father's house
and country. Even so shall it be with her, the hand
of the Lord will overrule it for good to her and her
father's family."

Turning to the young girl he continued:

"Sister Lydia, great are your blessings. The Lord,
your Savior, loves you, and will overrule all your
past sorrows and afflictions for good unto you.
Let your heart be comforted. You are of the blood
of Israel descended through the loins of Ephraim.
You shall yet be a savior to your father's house.
Therefore, be comforted, and let your heart
rejoice, for the Lord has a great work for you to
do. Be faithful and endure unto the end and all
will be well."

Lydia gathered with the Saints to Kirtland. There she met
Newel Knight, a widower. He "was tall, had light brown
hair, a keen blue eye and a very energetic and determined
manner." Love grew between them, but when Newel
proposed marriage Lydia was indignant. Notwithstanding
her husband's three year absence, Lydia was still married.
She could not marry again.

Distressed, Newel took the matter to Joseph and Joseph
took it to the Lord. Lydia was free to marry, the Lord

said, and such a union would please him. Filled with joy, Lydia threw herself upon her knees and poured out her soul in thanks to God. She consented to marry Newel and within days, word reached her that her former husband was dead.

On November 23, 1835, Lydia and Newel were married by Joseph Smith the Prophet, the first marriage he had ever performed.

Time passed and theirs was a happy, fulfilling union. Children came, and the family moved with the saints from Kirtland to Missouri, to Nauvoo, and finally onto the plains of Iowa in the Mormon exodus.

At a place called Ponca Camp in northern Nebraska, on Christmas Day 1846, a fire swept down on the Saints, threatening to destroy all they built. Newel and others fought the fire to the ground. By 11:00 that night, they had put it out—but at a terrible cost. Newel contracted pneumonia.

On January 1, 1847 Newel wrote in his journal the following:

> "I scarcely know why I am thus anxious, why this world appears so trifling, or the things of this world. I almost desire to leave this tenement of clay, that my spirit may soar aloft and no longer be held in bondage, yet my helpless family seem to need my protection. For their sake, and if I yet have more to do on earth, or can do more good to the living than to the dead, I am willing to remain yet longer in the flesh. Thy will, O Lord be done and not mine."

On January 11, 1847, Lydia, "sat with tightly closed hands and wild, agonized eyes, watching the breath of the being she loved better than life itself slowly cease.

"Lydia," the dying voice faintly whispered, "it is necessary for me to go. Joseph wants me. It is needful that a messenger be sent with the true condition of the Saints. Don't grieve too much, for you will be protected."

"Oh Newel, don't speak so; don't give up; oh I could not bear it. Think of me, Newel, here in an Indian country alone, with seven little children. No resting place for my feet, no one to counsel, to guide, or to protect me. I cannot let you go."

The dying man looked at her for a moment, and then said with a peculiar look: "I will not leave you now Lydia."

But, he was in such terrible agony. When she could bear his suffering no longer, Lydia knelt and prayed that if it really was the will of the Lord, let him go.

> "The prayer was scarcely over ere a calm settled on the sufferer, and with one long, loving look in the eyes of his beloved wife, the shadow lifted and the spirit fled."

That evening, Newel was buried. No lumber could be had, so Lydia had one of her wagon boxes made into a rude coffin. The day was excessively cold, and some of the brethren had their fingers and feet frozen while digging the grave and performing the last offices of love for their honored captain and brother.

As the woman looked out upon the wilderness of snow and saw the men bearing away all that was left of her husband, it seemed that the flavor of life had fled and left only dregs, bitter unavailing sorrow. But as she grew calmer, she whispered with poor, pale lips, "God rules." Lydia joined the other saints at Winter Quarters to prepare for the move west. She attended the organization meeting, overwhelmed at the enormity of it all. How could she, with seven children, make a 1000 mile journey into the wilderness?

The burden weighed her spirit down until she cried out in her pain, "Oh Newel, why hast thou left me!"

As she spoke, he stood by her side, with a lovely smile on his face, and said:

> "Be calm, let not sorrow overcome you. It was necessary that I should go. I was needed behind the veil to represent the true condition of this camp and people. You cannot fully comprehend it now; but the time will come when you shall know why I left you and our little ones. Therefore, dry up your tears. Be patient, I will go before you and protect you in your journeyings, and you and your little ones shall never perish for lack of food."

In time, Lydia and her children did make their way to Utah. When the St. George Temple opened in 1877, Lydia was called to be a temple worker, where she labored for the rest of her days, performing the sacred ordinances for hundreds of her kindred dead. Thus, she fulfilled the prophecy of Joseph that she would be a savior to her people.

We do not live and struggle alone. Those we love are just beyond the veil. God rules!

Source:
https://ancestors.familysearch.org/en/KWJP-CM6/lydia-goldthwaite-1812-1884

Mickey and Gypsy

It was the summer of 1912, near Tabiona, Utah. Rula Michie Wrigley, who was eight or nine at the time, wanted to go and visit a girlfriend who lived about two miles away. Rula was given permission and told to be home by dark.

The two little girls crossed the river and decided to climb a rock hill. It was evidently so much fun that they lost all track of time. Suddenly, they noticed that the sun was not only setting, but it was descending into black clouds. By the time they reached level ground, it was dark and the black clouds covered the sky.

Ella became frightened and ran for home, leaving Rula alone. Crying and scared, Rula started running for home with "only occasional flashes of lightning to show [her] way." She ran into some rocks and "fell sprawling." When she stood up, she "had lost all sense of direction." "I hadn't the faintest idea which direction to go," she said. There were no familiar landmarks anywhere.

Remembering what her mother had taught her about prayer, Rula knelt and asked "for help and guidance that [she] might reach home safely. When I finished my prayer," she said. "I stood up, and without any hesitation, I started walking. I still didn't know which direction I was going, but I had placed my trust in the Lord and felt that He would guide me."

As she walked along, limping in the threatening darkness, her hand swung to her side and brushed something furry. She said, "I was petrified with fear! It wasn't uncommon for people out there to meet coyotes, wolves, bears, cougars, etc. I thought one of them was about to devour me alive. I stayed in my tracks and stood perfectly still until the lightning flashed again. When I looked down, I saw a large dog looking up into my face. What a relief that was!

The dog licked my hand and I reached over and I got a good grip on the hair behind his ears. We started walking. I don't know how the dog knew where I was going, but he seemed to know. I was willing to follow him no matter where he took me. I figured there would at least be people there. He led me past a neighbor's place without even attempting to enter. I didn't see it, but knew we had passed it when the dog led me into our own gate and up to the house. We made it before the storm broke. Never was anyone more happy to reach home than I, in spite of the scolding I got for being so late."

The next morning, the dog was still there. No one recognized him. He didn't come from any of the neighboring ranches.

Because of that, she named him Gypsy, and he stayed. Rula said, "He used to go with me to school about halfway, and there he'd sit and watch me until I was out of sight. When I returned at night, he'd be there waiting for me. I don't know where he spent the time in between. If I were home alone, he wouldn't let anyone approach the house. He always accompanied me if I went hiking over the hills and was a most devoted friend and companion." In time, Rula was given the nickname of Mickey. They were Mickey and Gypsy— inseparable

companions. Then came the day that Rula went away to school.

Gypsy disappeared three days later, never to be seen again.

"I received help when I needed it," Rula said, "and it didn't matter whether the help came from an angel or from one of His humbler creatures, a dog."

Source:
Story contributed by Dallin Wrigley

https://www.familysearch.org/tree/person/memories/KWC6-14L

53
Chapter Fifty-Three

Miracle of the Seagulls

In the spring of 1848, pioneers in the Salt Lake Valley eagerly planted their crops. However, late frosts killed some of the plants and a lack of rain killed more of them. Then crickets came and attacked the plants that were needed for food to sustain them through the winter months. For two weeks, the pioneers did everything they could think of to fight the insects. The stake president finally asked the Saints to hold a special day of fasting and prayer. The answer to their prayers came on a clear summer afternoon, when great flocks of screaming seagulls descended.

Jesse Nathaniel Smith was a witness to this and wrote about what has come to be known as the miracle of the seagulls:

"Our corn and vegetables were large enough to show the rows nicely when the crickets appeared and commenced sweeping all before them in the way of [the] crops. We first turned the water in the ditches around the fields, but found that the crickets pushed boldly into the water without hesitancy or turning their course. Where the water was swift, they were washed down a long distance, but generally managed to reach the opposite bank. After lying in the sunshine awhile, [they] would fall to again, with as good an appetite as before. It seemed impossible to drown them, as they would recover after being a long time underwater.

They were very voracious, eating every green thing within their reach, but showing some preference for the dead or disabled of their own number....We endeavored to make headway against this new enemy, armed with sticks and clubs. All the people near us, male and female, turned out [to help]. We first went around outside the fields and killed enough [of the crickets] for the others to eat while we went over the patches, row by row, and killed all we saw. When we began again at the border, a little before dusk, the creatures went to roost upon the bushes or clustered under [dirt] clods for the night, only to renew the attack as soon as the sun appeared above the mountains. It was wearisome work contending against such fearful odds, but help was near.

We had thus fought ....[for] days, when great flocks of while gulls from beyond the lake appeared in our fields. Finding they made common cause with us against the crickets, we withdrew and left to them the honors. Their appetite for the crickets seemed as great as that of the crickets for our growing crops...., for when the gulls had filled themselves, they would seek the water ditches, and after drinking, disgorge themselves upon the ground and immediately return to fill themselves again.... In a few days, the crickets were exterminated, and the gulls withdrew toward the setting sun to return no more. Can it be wondered that we looked with affection upon our deliverers, with

their pretty eyes and dainty feet? They saved the crops for the infant colony."

In honor of this miracle, the seagull monument was erected on Temple Square in Salt Lake City, Utah in 1913. It shows two bronze seagulls on top of a granite column. On it are four raised panels that tell the story of the crickets and the seagulls. On one of the four raised panels it says, "Erected in grateful remembrance of the mercy of God to the Mormon pioneers."

Prayers are not always answered in the way we expect. Even the most unlikely help, sent as common birds, can be an instrument in the Lord's hands to help and preserve his children.

Source:
https://www.familysearch.org/tree/person/memories/KWCX-4KH

The Journal of Jesse Nathaniel Smith 1834-1906. Second printing 1997. P.13

https://www.churchofjesuschrist.org/study/history/topics/crickets-and-seagulls?lang=eng

Mother Whitmore and the Angel

It is one of the most sacred sites of Mormonism—the Peter Whitmer Cabin in Fayette, New York. It was here that the Book of Mormon translation was completed. It was here that three men were chosen as special witnesses and granted the opportunity to converse with an angel, view the plates, and hear the witness of God in regards to The Book of Mormon. It was also here that The Church of Jesus Christ of Latter-day Saints was organized on April 6, 1830, and many other great revelations were received. Considering the incalculable souls eternally blessed by what happened here, truly this is a holy place where the mercy of God was abundant.

There was a day when this glorious future almost didn't happen here. Joseph Smith came to Fayette in June 1829, at the encouragement of Peter and Mary Whitmer—whose home and farm it was. It was their generosity that opened up an upper room in which to translate. It was the food at their table and a place to sleep that sustained life while the work progressed. With Joseph came Emma and Oliver, as well as an innumerable train of visitors and the curious. All of this added to the burden on Mother Whitmer, who felt the responsibility to care for them.

One day she was particularly tired. She went outside to attend to the evening chores and milk the cow. She saw Joseph and Oliver nearby skating rocks across the pond—an activity they often did to relax and relieve the tedium of translation. It annoyed her and she

thought to herself that they might just chop some wood or carry a bucket of water as skate rocks, and according to her family, she was about to order them from the home.

She came out of the barn carrying two buckets of milk, when she was met by a stranger—an old man, heavy set, with a knapsack on his back. At first, she was frightened, but the record states:

> "When he spoke to her in a kind, friendly tone and began to explain to her the nature of the work which was going on in her house, she was filled with inexpressible joy and satisfaction. He then untied his knapsack and showed her a bundle of plates, which in size and appearance corresponded with the description subsequently given by the witnesses to The Book of Mormon. This strange person turned the leaves of the book of plates over, leaf after leaf, and also showed her the engravings upon them; after which he told her to be patient and faithful in bearing her burden a little longer, promising that if she would do so, she should be blessed; and her reward would be sure, if she proved faithful to the end. The personage then suddenly vanished with the plates, and where he went, she could not tell. From that moment [Mother Whitmer] was enabled to perform her household duties with comparative ease, and she felt no more inclination to murmur because her lot was hard."

Source:

Taken from an article by Royal Skousen in Interpreter: A Journal of Mormon Scripture 10 (2014)

A Traveler's Protection

Cyrus Wheelock joined the Church in 1839 and was faithful all his days. He was in Carthage in June 1844 and warned Governor Thomas Ford of the plot to assassinate Joseph Smith. When his warnings were unheeded, Cyrus slipped a pistol to Joseph in the cell. On the morning of the martyrdom, it was Cyrus that Joseph asked to carry a letter to Emma in Nauvoo.

After serving as a missionary from 1846-1853, Cyrus was appointed to lead a company of saints across the plains to Salt Lake in 1853. In 1854, he was immediately called out once more to serve. It was while returning from that service in England, that Cyrus volunteered and went back out onto the plains to rescue the stranded handcart saints of 1856.

Cyrus lived in Lehi and in Springville, but eventually settled with his large family in Mt. Pleasant, Utah. It was while living there that his family tells of this experience.

Cyrus was one day traveling from Mt. Pleasant to Fairview, Utah—a distance of 5-6 miles. Outside of town, he happened upon a stranger who asked for a ride into Fairview. Cyrus agreed and the man climbed up into the back of the buggy. As they went along, they noticed Indians lying in wait along the road, hiding in the tall grass. Cyrus was about to turn back when the stranger urged him to keep going since they were halfway there. Cyrus agreed and they continued

on. Just then, very strange things began to happen in the heavens. "All kinds of cloud formations began to take place. It held the Indians attention until they had arrived safely at Fairview."

Once past the danger, Cyrus turned back to talk to the stranger but "He had disappeared without a sound. Cyrus firmly believed the stranger was one of the Three Nephites sent to protect him."

Source:
https://www.familysearch.org/tree/person/memories/KWJ4-D4R

Sarah Farr and the Stranger

Sarah Farr had just finished cleaning her kitchen after the family's midday meal when she heard a firm knock at the back door of her home. Her family lived at 23 North West Temple in Salt Lake City, where the Family History Library now stands. The year was about 1878.

When she opened the door, there stood a man who appeared to be poor, but was tidy-looking. It was not unusual for strangers such as this to come to her door, as she lived not too far east of the train station. The man asked for something to eat. So often did strangers come by looking for help like this that Sarah's husband, John Henry, had purchased meal tickets that the family would provide to such strangers where they could get a good meal at a nearby restaurant.

However, there was something different about this man and Sarah invited him in. He took a seat at her kitchen table and she served him some food. As he was eating, he suddenly asked where her son was. She responded by telling him that the lad was outside playing in the yard. He then asked her to call him into the house. He wanted to see him.

Sarah was hesitant. This man was a stranger and she did not want to leave him alone in the house. Nevertheless, there was something about him that caused her to comply with his request. She went out back and found her son, playing underneath a second-story balcony at a building just north of her home.

She called him and he came. Together they went back to the house. When they entered, the stranger was gone. They searched through the home, but he was nowhere to be found. Then, suddenly, there came a loud crash. Mother and son ran outside to investigate and discovered that the balcony under which the lad had been playing just moments before had collapsed. Large beams and heavy timbers had fallen to the ground and crushed the toys the boy had left behind. Had he still been there, he would not have survived.

That inspired and obedient mother was Sarah Farr Smith and that little boy was George Albert Smith, the eighth president of The Church of Jesus Christ of Latter-day Saints.

Source:

Story contributed by Susan Arrington Madsen

The story originates from oral history delivered by W. Whit Smith, a grandson of Sarah and John Henry, on 2 May 1986, to Susan Arrington Madsen.

She Wants Us to Stay

William and Mary Penfold Goble joined The Church of Jesus Christ of Latter-day Saints in March 1855. They sold their home and business and paid for their passage to Zion. On May 19, 1856, they sailed for America on the ship Horizon. Upon their arrival in America, they rode by train to Iowa, where they were assigned to the Hunt Wagon Company. As they waited to depart, their youngest child, Fanny, died. The company left Iowa City August 1, 1856. It was Sept 23, 1856, when Sister Goble delivered a baby girl whom they named Edith. The little one only lived about six weeks and then died from lack of nourishment. She was buried on the banks of the Sweetwater River. When the snow came, the company suffered from exposure and starvation.

On December 11, 1856, between Big and Little Mountains, Mother Mary Penfold Goble passed away. She had not been well since the birth of her baby Edith. She was only forty-three years old. The family, frozen and barely alive, made it into Salt Lake City at 9:00 p.m. on December 11, 1856. The next morning, President Brigham Young brought a doctor with him and upon meeting the family and seeing their pitiful condition wept and exclaimed, "My God! This is the worst I have ever seen."

Shortly after, the family moved to Nephi where they bought a lot and built an adobe home. According to his biographers:

"He was not used to the life he now had to live, which was much different from life in England. During the summer, he became very discouraged and told the children that he would take them back home to England as soon as he could earn enough money. At the time, he was working at the lime kiln. Some time later, he came home one day and said to the children, 'I have seen your mother today. She wants us to stay here [and] everything will be alright.'"

William Goble stayed, raised his family, and is buried in Nephi, Utah. Thank the Lord for an angel mother who came and encouraged Father Goble to stay. His family grew up in the faith. He left a legacy of healing and faith, and noble posterity that continue to honor his memory—among whom was Marjorie Pay Hinckley, the wife of Gordon B. Hinckley. Just think of how things might have been different if William's angel wife had not appeared.

Source:
https://www.familysearch.org/tree/person/details/KWJ8-R57

Chapter Fifty-Eight

They Will Take Care of You

In 1985, Terry Tullis accompanied his family, along with another family, for a grand adventure touring Europe. The group purchased 30-day Eurail European Rail passes to be able to ride an unlimited number of miles through 33 European countries. They had a general plan of where they wanted to travel, but knew the itinerary would need to be flexible. Their vacation started in England, then across the English Channel on a hydrofoil ship to Belgium. From there, they traveled to Bern, Switzerland to visit the Swiss Temple. The adults and teens were prompted to stay longer than planned and assist a large group of members from Spain in doing temple work that day. Terry said, "The Spirit was so strong it seemed as if we were transformed to a higher level of spirituality we had never experienced before." By staying later at the temple, they were too late to board the train leaving for Germany and spent an additional night in Switzerland.

The travelers left for Germany early the next morning, arriving in the early afternoon. They thought it was strange that the train stopped about 100 yards from the main station. The group got off the train and learned there had a been a tragic bombing at the station the evening before which killed one person and injured several others. Terry said, "I was suddenly aware.... that had we not been delayed by staying at the Swiss Temple, that the original time of our arrival at this.... station would have closely coincided with the time of the bomb blast. There was no doubt in my heart [that]

the Lord was involved withthis…".

As they traveled further north in Germany, they were a
bit naïve as to the travel limitations of the rail system.
They arrived in the town of Garmisch on the last train
north for the day. They disembarked and suddenly
realized they were the only two families left waiting on
the platform. Seeing three hotels not far from the train
station, Terry went to each one and was told they had
no vacancies. Downcast and worried, he returned to the
waiting families praying, "Heavenly Father, what do I do
now?"

After a few moments, a medium sized man who spoke
English with a slight accent "seemed to come out of
nowhere" and stopped in front of the two worried
fathers. The man asked, "Are you looking for a place to
stay for the night?" They replied, "Yes." He said, "Come
with me." After walking about 100 feet, he pointed out
a hotel and said, "You go over there. It's inexpensive
and they will take care of you." He then pointed to a
different hotel and said, "That hotel is very expensive.
You don't want to go there." Terry tried to explain that
he had already checked both hotels and tried to thank
the stranger for his kindness, but he just seemed to have
disappeared.

Without much hope, Terry proceeded to the suggested
hotel, where the male receptionist greeted him as if he
had never seen him before. He was told they didn't have
any rooms, but after a long silence the clerk said, "The
owner of this hotel has a large apartment in the rear of
the hotel and he is away for several weeks. You can have
his apartment." Terry brought his group from the
train platform and they were shown a beautiful, clean

apartment with "rooms and beds for all nine of us." Terry related:

> "It was truly a miracle. I suddenly knew we had an encounter with an angel that night. I have never ever forgotten that moment nor how I felt. Over the years, as I have read and reread the trip journal, I have realized over and over again how involved the protection of the Lord was with us, including the encounter with an angel that night."

Source:
Story contributed by Terry Tullis

59

Stardust

One evening back in the late 90's, I was meditating with my eyes closed and listening to native American music. I suddenly felt a presence from the other side of the veil and knew immediately it was a loved one who had passed. It was clear that whoever it was wanted desperately to push through the veil and communicate with me.

I wasn't sure it was "appropriate" to ask, but I felt such anxiousness from the being on the other side that I said a short, intense prayer, pleading with Heavenly Father to let whoever it was on the other side of the veil to pass through. Instantly, our horse, Stardust, whom we had to put down a few years before because of liver disease, burst through the veil and into my presence.

She had always been my favorite of all our horses, the one I felt most connected to. I was startled at first because I expected it to be one of my ancestors, but in the same instant was filled with overwhelming love and joy. She expressed what joy she had in being our horse and how grateful she was for our earthly experiences together. I was sobbing great sobs of joy, but my wife heard me and rushed to me, fearing that something was wrong. As she did so, the "vision" faded, but I was still so overwhelmed with emotion that it took me several seconds to compose myself enough to be able to assure her that everything was all right. In fact, I had never felt that everything was more all right than I did at that moment.

As I came down from that celestial high, I thought of Joseph F. Smith's vision of his father, Hyrum, and his Uncle Joseph riding the streets of heaven on their favorite horses. I give thanks that there are no insignificant relationships in our Heavenly Father's eyes, and that ALL the relationships we enjoy here will endure in full felicity throughout eternity.

Source:
Story contributed by Scott Fullmer

60
Chapter Sixty

The Big Pioneer Greyhound

Our God is a God of miracles!

Henry Tempest and his family left England in 1860 to come to America. They pulled a handcart in the Daniel Robison Company. It was not long after Henry left Florence, Nebraska that he became so ill that the Captain requested Henry return to Florence. However, Henry had not come all this way to stop now. More than anything, he wanted to go on, and so he begged the Captain to let him stay just one more day to see if he would get better.

> That night, Henry poured out his heart to the Lord and explained how much he wanted to go on and would the Almighty somehow help him get to Utah. The following morning, Henry felt somewhat improved—at least enough that he could help his two young sons pull the handcart.

When they made camp that night, Henry rested while his family took care of the evening chores.

According to the account:

"That night, a large greyhound dog came into camp. It ran from one group to another until it came to the little camp Henry and his boys had made. After it sniffed around, it lay down and seemed to be at home. The boys were delighted. They talked to it and petted it."

However, pets were not allowed. If the animal did not work, there was not sufficient food for it.

Henry had an idea. He rigged up a harness and put it on the dog. Strangely, the dog didn't seem to mind. In fact, he acted as though he had done this before. He pulled the handcart all the next day, and the next, and the next....Hundreds of miles across the plains, that faithful dog pulled the handcart. Oh, how they loved that big greyhound.

Finally, and joyfully, they came into the Salt Lake Valley—their new home. "A few days after they arrived, the big pioneer greyhound disappeared and was never seen again."

This is just a simple reminder of the goodness of God.

Source:
"A Dog to Pull Their Handcart", Instructor, May 1962, p. 147.

The Book of Mormon Is a True Record

In December 1832, Joseph Smith and Jared Carter came to the area around Pontiac, Michigan preaching the Gospel. One of the families that Joseph visited was the family of Nahum and Millicent Curtis. According to family records this is the account of their visit:

> "A meeting was held at my father's house. That night after retiring, the parents were conversing upon the principles they had just listened to for the first time, when they noticed the room begin to grow light. It grew lighter and lighter until it was as bright as noonday. Then they heard a voice say, 'Nahum, the Book of Mormon is a true record of the people that lived on this continent.'"

The family was converted, and in time, each of them joined the Church, as did some seventy others. In 1834, when Hyrum Smith led a group of recruits from Pontiac to join Zion's Camp on the march to Missouri, Nahum and Millicent's son, Lyman Curtis, were among those who volunteered. When Zion's Camp was disbanded, Lyman and his new bride, Charlotte Alvord, chose to stay in Missouri. When the saints were driven from the State of Missouri by the mobs, Lyman and Charlotte were among those who made the flight between January and March 1839.

At one particular river crossing, the water had risen and their wagon was swept downstream from the ford. Their horses were unable to find good footing and couldn't pull

the wagon out of the water. Finally, men came to help them and they were able to get the wagon across the river. The account continues:

> "About an hour after they got out, one of the horses, "Old Claybank," named for his color, laid down and died. Many people gathered around the dead horse, expressing sympathy. A tall man reached through the crowd and said, 'Mr. Curtis, here is thirty-five dollars, go and buy another horse.' Lyman was so surprised that for a minute he could only look at the money in his hand. When he turned to thank him, the man was nowhere to be seen. Even though the crowd helped look for him, he was not found. No one had seen him come or go. With the money, they were able to buy a horse as good as the one that was lost."

Lyman Curtis and his family were faithful members of the church. He helped in the building of the Kirtland and Nauvoo temples and was one of Joseph Smith's bodyguards. Family records relate that Lyman was blessed by Joseph Smith, who uttered the singular prophecy that he would "strike the rock and bring forth water." Lyman was part of Brigham Young's original company who arrived in the valley in 1847. He returned to the east and brought his family to settle in Utah, where Joseph's prophecy was fulfilled, as he worked to develop irrigation canals and bring water to communities in Utah.

Source:
https://www.familysearch.org/tree/person/memories/KWNV-RZP

https://www.familysearch.org/tree/person/memories/KWNL-NRS

The Conversion of Luman Shurtliff

Luman Andros Shurtliff was born March 13, 1807, the fifth and youngest child of Noah and Lydia Brown Shurtliff. While still a lad, Luman developed a love of God. He would say of himself:

> "Secretly, I was a Christian as far as I knew, but kept it entirely to myself, yet went by myself and prayed continually, hoping the time would come soon when I could join some church and have young people for my brothers and sisters."

When he and his brothers would go out to the sugar camp to harvest maple sap, Luman walked in his brother Selah's tracks in the snow and no other, "Because he was a Christian" and acted like it. If Selah was there, Luman felt safe.

Beginning in 1832, Luman became aware of The Church of Jesus Christ of Latter-day Saints there in Ohio. One night he experienced a dream that only a farmer could appreciate. He said:

> "I dreamed. I thought I was standing in the northeast corner of my room. It was as light as day but not daylight. I could see plain and clear. I stood facing the east. I stooped forward and had a large-sized hog by the nose and was examining it. It was a white hog, but dirty. One ear was close to the head. The other was off one inch from the head and the tail was also gone.

The hair was long and very rough looking. It had a well-built frame, but was very poor. When I was through looking at this hog, I looked a little to the northeast and there stood another white hog, perfect in every part. Its beauty exceeded in every part any hog I ever saw. This hog stood, its head up and looking toward Kirtland.

In the morning when we awoke, I told Eunice (his wife) I had dreamed a rather singular dream and this dream seemed to show that The Book of Mormon was quite inferior to the Bible. I told her of my dream. 'Why,' said Eunice, 'I should think it was the Bible that was inferior.' As quick as though the scene changed, and the two hogs represented the two books. The Bible [was] poor, lean, disfigured, and robbed by translators of many of its precious parts [and] The Book of Mormon, white and pure from the hand of the Almighty and perfect in all its parts, like all the work of God. In a short time, I began to think it was a dream, and could I rest my salvation on a dream? I should be ashamed to have people know I had left my religion and embraced another because I had dreamed about a couple of hogs. So the devil reasoned with me until I became so confused, I concluded to wait and see what further evidence I could get before I joined the Mormons."

The dreams and encounters with the church continued, but Luman remained troubled and unconvinced. Then in August 1836, Luman determined he would journey to Kirtland, "The seat of Mormonism" he called it, to see if he "could find out the truth or falsity of this

doctrine from there." There he found no peace. His mind was darkened with doubts and his body shook with torment of soul. "I would be standing on some eminence weeping like a whipped child and I knew no reason why." He wandered about the city "like a man of little sense." He went to David Whitmer, the Witness, who bore his testimony and listened while Luman shared his doubts and fears.

"I could not say that I believed that Joseph Smith, Jr. was a true prophet of God, for I did not. Neither did I believe The Book of Mormon to be a revelation from God, for I did not. Then facing him I said, 'Now you know what I believe and what I do not believe, and if you think I am a fit subject for baptism, I am ready to go to the water; if not, I intend to start home tomorrow and never trouble my head any more about Mormonism.' Mr. Whitmer was silent for a few seconds and then replied, 'I will go to the water and baptize you or get one of my quorum to do it.' On the way to the river, he called on Sylvester Smith and at sunset on Sunday, August 21, 1836, I was baptized a member of the Church. David Whitmer confirmed me."

As Luman started home he took stock. Did he now believe? What would he tell his neighbors and friends when he got back?

"Did I believe the Book of Mormon? No. No more than I did four years ago. Do I believe that Joseph Smith, Jr. is a prophet of God? No, I do not. At this I was shocked at my situation and began to call on the Lord in earnest. While I was praying, something came on my head, resembling cold water, and passed gradually down through my whole system, removing all pain (He had for some time been crippled and in great pain), and made me a sound man from the top of my head to the soles of my feet. As soon as this was passed, I heard a sweet, melodious voice about me say, 'Joseph Smith, Jr. is a prophet of the Most High God, raised up for the restoration of Israel in these last days, and The Book of Mormon which you hold under your arm is true and brought forth for the restoration of the scattered remnants of Jacob.'"

By the power of the Holy Ghost, Luman Andros Shurtliff was converted and true and faithful would prove it the rest of his days.

Source:
http://www.boap.org/LDS/Early-Saints/LShurtliff.html

63

Chapter Sixty-Three

The Eagle

When Donnell was just a lad in the Boy Scouts, he
developed a love of birds that lasted
throughout his life. Everywhere he went, he carried his
bird identification books and binoculars.
He kept a daily log of the birds he saw. Truly he loved
the winged creations and over his life
identified close to a thousand different species of birds.

His family remembers fondly the annual family May
Day event, where Donnell would load them
up and lead them into the field at the advent of spring
to see how many birds they could see in a day.

As any will know who appreciate the hand of the
Almighty in the Creation, this was not just a
lifelong passion, but a spiritual experience of great joy.

Then on February 4, 2013, at the age of 82, Don
passed away quietly. As friends and family came to
pay their last respects, they were handed a program
outlining the order of events. Notable on that program
was the image of a bald eagle.

At the close of the services later that day, on the way
back from the cemetery, Don's beloved
wife, Nita, noticed off to the left of the car, flying
alongside them—a bald eagle. It would veer to
the left and then back to the road, then off to the right
and back once again, but he stayed with
them. This majestic bird escorted Nita until just before

she arrived at the church, when he winged away and was gone.

Nita later told me, "It was as though Don had sent the eagle as a sign that he was still there
watching over me and letting me know of his love and concern for me in his absence."

Praise God for his tender mercies.

64

Chapter Sixty-Four

The Gate

It was early summer, 1916, near Tabiona in eastern Utah. The ward Relief Society President, Esther Wagstaff, decided she wanted to pay a visit to those sisters who lived across the river who had been shut in by winter snows and bad roads. She asked one of her counselors to go with her, Elena Dorothy Lambert Michie. The two of them climbed in the wagon and began their ministering journey of love and duty.

As the day progressed, they traveled from sister to sister,making their visits. Each time they came to a gate to someone's property, Sister Michie would climb down, open it, wait for Sister Wagstaff to drive the wagon through, and then would close it and climb back up in the wagon. Now, for a pioneer woman in her sixties that's a chore, especially for one suffering from severe varicose veins. Elena, or 'Grandma Lena' as her family referred to her, said:

> "Well, we turned homeward, and of course,
> there were the gates to go through again, but
> we didn't talk of that. I just climbed out of the
> wagon and opened each gate as we came to it,
> and when Sister Wagstaff had driven through,
> I closed the gate again and got back into
> the wagon. As we neared the last gate, Sister
> Wagstaff said, 'Hasn't this been a satisfying day?
> It has been so good to visit these sisters.'

I said, "Yes, it's been a wonderful day. Now if we just didn't have to open anymore gates!"

To our amazement, the gate just ahead of us opened by itself. The heavy piece of two by four that went from the gate into the gate posts moved by itself and the gate swung open. I had dragged it open a few hours before. Sister Wagstaff drove through. One of us said in a whisper, 'Let's watch and see if it closes.' We both turned around and watched as the gate swung shut and was fastened.

I just can't tell you how we felt. I guess it was a miracle right before our eyes. Those gates were heavy. You know how they were made, poles and two by fours and barbed wire. Well, we had done the best we could to do our duty. Maybe our guardian angels were there to help. I just don't know."

The Lord once said, "I will go before your face. I will be on your right hand and on your left, and my Spirit shall be in your hearts, and mine angels round about you to bear you up" (Doctrine and Covenants 84:88). And so they are!

Source:
https://www.familysearch.org/tree/person/memories/KWCF-4V5

The Miracle Loaf of Bread

James Fisher left a wife and three children to answer a call to serve as a missionary in New Zealand. For three years and four months, he served faithfully, while his wife ran the farm, raised the children, and worked diligently to support him.

One day, while Elder Fisher and his companion were riding along on their horses, they started talking about home, as missionaries will often do. "They talked about how much they missed the good, homemade bread so common back in Utah. Money from home had not yet arrived and they were, quite simply, hungry.

Elder Fisher's companion suggested that they were alone and could dismount. They went into the woods and prayed. They expressed their desire to serve, as well as their love and concern for those back home. The two elders felt better, got back on their horses, and continued on their way. As they rode along, they noticed something just off the road.

They dismounted, and to their amazement, found wrapped in a white cloth, a fresh loaf of bread, the same kind of homemade bread they had talked about in their prayer. They rejoiced as they ate it, although it wasn't the bread that was so important, but the reassurance that Heavenly Father knew who they were and where they were, that they had faithful wives and that the Lord's kindness and goodness was over them all."

Of course, both missionaries wrote home and told their wives of the miracle. Postage was expensive and mail traveled slowly. About three months after the event, Elder Fisher's companion received a letter from his wife. She told him that on the day they received their miracle loaf of bread "she had been baking bread, and when she opened the oven to take it out, one of the pans was empty and a white cloth that had been on the table was gone."

Two humble missionaries received a tender mercy from the Lord.

> "The loaf of bread came to symbolize for them that it was Heavenly Father who had sent them to New Zealand and that he was supporting and watching over their families. Incidentally, when James E. returned home, the farm had prospered and he and his wife owned more cattle and sheep and had more money than before . . . . Because of their willingness to sacrifice in the service of the Lord, they received miraculous blessings."

Source:

Story Contributed by Dorcas Anderson. James Fisher was her Great Grandfather.

Elder Ted E. Brewerton, New Era, November 1990

https://www.familysearch.org/tree/person/memories/KWCX-DCX

The Whitewashed Wall

The story is told by the descendants of Margaret
Crawford of a most unusual event in about
1842. Margaret lived in Lanarkshire, Scotland. In those
days, folks relied heavily on the burning
of coal, which could quickly turn everything black. In
the Crawford home, they had a large
fireplace at one end of a low ceiling room, where the
family did most of their cooking. There
were large deposits of chalk in the hills nearby which
could be mixed with water to make a
functional white-wash that was used to "paint" the
walls. It was Margaret's job to do the painting,
as she was the oldest girl. According to the account of
Margaret's granddaughter:

> "She had just finished her task and was
> admiring the snow-white walls and hoping it
> would not have to be done again very soon.
> A knock came at the door and she went and
> opened it and let in what seemed to be a beggar.
> He walked into the room and looked at the
> girl and at the mother and the white walls. He
> stood a moment and gazed steadily at Margaret.
> He then walked to the fireplace and picked up
> a piece of charcoal, went to the white walls,
> and began to write. The mother and daughter
> looked on in speechless amazement. No one
> had uttered a word since the appearance of
> this strange person. Then both Margaret and
> her mother began to remonstrate at having the

walls all marked up with black charcoal. But, he would not quit and seemed to know nothing of what they were saying. He continued writing until he had covered the whole wall from top to bottom. When he had finished, he walked from the room, never saying a word."

According to another account, when the stranger had finished, he went outside. Margaret and her mother went out right after. The stranger was nowhere to be seen, nor had the children playing there seen him. Margaret and her mother went back inside to see what the man had written. It was a message to Margaret declaring that:

"Margaret was going to be visited by a young man who was teaching a new and strange religion. This young man was from the new world and had crossed many waters to teach her their religion. She would accept their new religion and some of her family would, but others would not accept, and she would suffer persecution by joining it. The young man, who was of her own nationality, would return to her home, then he would come again to her land and take her as his wife across the many waters. There in the new world they would build a home and have a great posterity."

The family laughed and made fun of the message. It was just a fairy tale. Not long after, a young man by the name of James Houston, originally from Paisley, Scotland, who had been called as a missionary for The Church of Jesus Christ of Latter-day Saints in Nauvoo, came into the area. He taught Margaret the gospel,

baptized her in the River Clyde, and married her shortly after.

After Elder Houston's release in 1845, the couple sailed for America, arriving in Nauvoo just in time for the great exodus of the Saints to the Rocky Mountains. James and Margaret settled in St George, Utah and were blessed with nine children.

Source:

https://www.familysearch.org/tree/person/memories/KWBB-6WN

https://www.familysearch.org/tree/person/memories/KWBB-6WJ

67
Chapter Sixty-Seven
The Work for the Dead

If anyone doubts that we live after we die or that the spirit world is closely connected to this one, please consider these experiences of Joseph Stacy Murdock. He tells of a time when he and other family members were doing work for the dead in the temple in St. George. Joseph said:

"I was the last one dressing and came out of the dressing rooms into the baptismal chamber. Here stood three ladies, side by side. One of them spoke to me and said, 'Here are three of your aunts that you have missed in your work.' I did not know them. They had died before I knew them. ...I...found my sister Betsy. She was 15 years older than myself, and told her that we had missed three of our aunts. She thought not. I told her we would look over the papers. We did so and soon found the three aunts we had missed, and I had their work done. I bear my testimony that I saw them with my natural eyes and heard their voices with my ears."

On another occasion, presumably, somewhere near the end of his life Joseph described seeing his father, long-since-deceased, in a dream.

"He came to me one night and told me that he would give me until ten o'clock on the third day to live on the earth. I understood I would have to die and leave my family, children and all. It seemed to me I never could have had anything more real come to me. After all my thoughts, I told Father that I had no excuse to make, if

he said, "go", go it was, but there was one thing
I had thought of, and I did not know that I was
worthy to carry it out. He stopped and studied
me and said, 'What is it, Joseph?' I said it was in
relation to our dead that I would be willing to do
for them all, if I could. He then said he would see
me again about that. He returned to me again that
same night and told me I had better tarry on the
earth, but he was very busy and needed me very
much, and I woke up. So you see, the dead have
something to do. I had one of my sons die, by
the name of Nymphas Hyrum Murdock. He was
killed by a log in the Provo River. I am satisfied he
is with my father in the Spirit World."

And lastly, what is it that the dead have to do once they
have died? Joseph, who obviously had the spiritual gift of
dreams and revelations, said this:

"My brother John, who is dead, came to me in
a dream. He stood at my bedside, looking very
anxious for me to speak to him. I spoke to him.
I said, 'John, are you perfectly happy?' 'No,' was
his reply, 'nor no man can be when he first leaves
this earth.' 'I will explain myself by saying when
we were little boys, we had to learn our letters,
beginning with a, b, c, and so on. When we pass
through the veil into the Spirit World, we go by
degrees from one to another and so on. I don't
want you and mother to worry any more about
me. I am a great deal better off than I was on
earth. I have had power given me to waft myself
from one place to another. For that reason, I have
come to see you and tell you that it takes time for
perfect happiness.'"

This is one man's experiences with the world beyond. He speaks of those who lived true and faithful on the earth. His dreams are consistent with the Lord's doctrines, as taught by the prophets. For us, it is simple—keep the commandments, be true to this work, and get ready.

Source:

https://www.familysearch.org/tree/person/memories/KWJD-VKH

This Is the One

The year was 1901, when friends invited a young college student who was living in Oslo, Norway to a concert sponsored by members of The Church of Jesus Christ of Latter-day Saints. His name was Torlief Knaphus. He was impressed and began attending meetings. Shortly after, he was baptized a member. He was a gifted art major and was offered a scholarship to study in Rome. Instead, in 1905, he chose to emigrate to Utah. Once there, his talent was recognized and he was commissioned over the years to work on the Salt Lake Tabernacle and temples in Salt Lake City, Utah, Laie, Hawaii, Cardston, Alberta, Idaho Falls, Idaho, Mesa, Arizona, and Los Angeles, California. It is very likely that you have admired the artistry of Torlief Knaphus somewhere in your travels.

When the Church acquired the Smith Farm and the Hill Cumorah in 1928, Torlief felt impressed that a monument needed to be raised to commemorate the beginnings of the Restoration. Accordingly, he prepared seven sketches of a statue to be raised on the Hill Cumorah. One night in 1929, he climbed to the top of Ensign Peak in Salt Lake City and spread the sketches out on the ground before him. He then prayed to know if he was doing the right thing. Would the brethren accept his idea? Which of the sketches was the right one?

"When he opened his eyes, there was a light all around him and he could see every one of the

seven sketches, even though it was dark. Then he
saw an angel pointing with his finger to the one
that he thought was the best and heard the angel
say, 'This is the one.' Torlief then asked, 'How
will I approach the Brethren? What will they
think? Have I done the right thing to do this?'
Then the angel said, 'You go to the Church
offices in the morning. They will be waiting for
you.'"

He met the brethren the next day and they
unanimously chose the one pointed to by the angel.
Torlief was commissioned to begin the work that would
take him five years to complete. Immediately, he began
his search for a model to sculpt. He found that model
in the physique of young Elwin Clark—a bricklayer
who had done some work for him. But though his
musculature was right, Torlief felt his face was too
young for the likeness of the Angel Moroni. He fasted
and prayed for help. Then one day, he was walking in
downtown Salt Lake City and saw a man who struck
him as the perfect model. He followed him and studied
his features. Finally, he approached him and asked if he
would be willing to model for this unique sculpture.
The man was a rancher from Wyoming, recently
returned to live in Salt Lake. He agreed and together
they walked back to Torlief's studio, which was not
far. When they walked in, Elwin Clarke, the young
bricklayer, was there. Can you imagine Torlief's surprise
when the two men knew each other? In fact, the older
gentleman was Hyrum Don Carlos Clark—Elwin
Clark's father.

The monument was dedicated on July 21, 1935 by
President Heber J. Grant. Today, each time I look up at
that beautiful statue, I am reverentially reminded, first,

of the sacred events of the coming forth of The Book of Mormon—of Moroni and the Prophet Joseph Smith, but secondly of the miracle of the monument itself— designed by revelation, chosen by the same angel and modeled by a miracle.

Source:

https://latterdaysaintmag.com/article-1-12275/

https://scholarsarchive.byu.edu/cgi/viewcontent. cgi?article=1367&context=jbms

https://www.churchofjesuschrist.org/inspiration/latter-day-saints- channel/listen/series/everything-creative-audio/church-sculptor-torleif- s-knaphus-discussion-50?lang=eng

69

Watched, Taken Care of, and Loved

It was June 1844, when 12 year old Henry Martin Harmon lived with his family in Carthage, Illinois. Henry's father and cousin had recently passed away while returning from missionary service. His mother had quickly remarried, and Henry was bitter and resentful, filled with grief, and wondering why. The family history of Henry Harmon records the following:

"He [Henry] remembered when they lived in Nauvoo how he had admired Joseph ... the Prophet Joseph. He wasn't hardly like a prophet ... at least a lot of folks wanted Joseph to be more like the Old Testament prophets, all fire and brimstone. He was mighty handsome and young and full of enthusiasm. But some folks were never happy with anything and criticized that Joseph was too handsome, young, and not sober enough to be fit for such a calling. Henry thought him mighty like a God. Henry, even then, had walked around in a daze from being uprooted and cast around. It seemed that Joseph understood. [There] Weren't many adults who went out of their way to talk to kids, but Joseph did. He'd wink sometimes when he couldn't leave a conversation to talk to Henry. When he did talk to Henry, he always asked after his Ma.

Joseph had a liking for people that went beyond what Henry had ever seen before. Henry could believe that Joseph was more a prophet than anybody else he could think of, but now Joseph was locked in the jail that stood across the street from his Ma's house ... the house Ma shared with Elias and his kids and Henry's brothers and sisters. It wasn't Henry's home that was for sure, just a place to sleep at night. He could see the jail now—the one Joseph was in. His Ma had taken Joseph some pie the other day, but the guard took it and she thought probably Joseph never got it. Henry stood still to think a minute. It didn't seem fair; it surely didn't. His Dad and cousin [were] dead for being a Mormon and Joseph locked in jail for the same thing—and his Ma always saying the Lord would watch after them.

The grief shook him again, just as he heard the shots and the commotion around the jail. He knew the trouble had finally come ... the trouble that everyone had been watchin' over their shoulders for and never knowing for sure when it would come. Henry saw Joseph leap from the window, one of the mob scream about revenge at last, and Joseph's body fall like a rag doll. Henry started to run. Some of the mob were in the dooryard of his Ma's house. She might be home alone and in trouble. He heard some of the eggs crack and felt goo run down on his hands. He threw the bag to the ground and ran faster. He'd have to worry about the cows after he found out how was his Ma.

It was then Henry saw the flash of light ... marking the passage of Joseph into heaven ... but was it really with his eyes he saw the light or with his heart? He trembled and brushed his wet cheeks. He felt an arm on his shoulder ... his

pa telling him that he must be a man now and take his place as a man in the family ... not to leave home as his brothers had done, because Ma needed him. Henry looked around but saw no one. He felt warm and the fear left him. There was that in him that knew he was being watched, taken care of, [and] loved."

Henry Martin Harmon eventually came west with his family and settled in Afton, Wyoming, where he passed away and is buried.

Source:
https://www.familysearch.org/tree/person/memories/KWZB-8Q8

70
We Felt Our Hearts Burn Within Us

Andrew Jackson Stewart and his companion, Amasa Potter, were serving as missionaries in New South Wales, Australia in 1857. Elder Potter recorded the following in his journal:

> "We received a letter from Emu Plains, stating that the people would like to see and hear a "Mormon" Elder. Emu Plains was a distance of sixty miles from where we were, and when we started, it had been raining for about a week, and a great portion of the country was flooded with water. We had a large river to cross on the way and were informed that the bridge had been carried off and there was a ferry established across the river which charged five shillings each passenger. We did not have any money with which to pay this charge, and my companion was anxious to know what we should do for money to pay for the ferriage. We were then about three miles from the ferry, and were passing through timber. I told him that we would go into the woods and pray to God to open the heart of someone to give it [the fare] to us.

> We did so, and we had traveled but a short distance through the lane between two fields, when we looked ahead of us a little way and saw an old man coming across the field. He came into the road ahead of us, and as he came to

meet us, he had a smile on his countenance. He reached out his hand to me, as if to shake hands, and left a crown, or five shilling piece, in my hand and went to my companion and did the same; but spoke not a word. I cannot describe the feeling that we had when the man took hold of our hands; we felt our hearts burn within us, and it did not seem that we had power to ask his name or where he was from, as we usually did when a person gave us any article of clothing or money. He was a man about six feet high, well proportioned, and wore a suit of light grey clothes and a broad-brimmed hat, and his hair and beard were about eighteen inches long and as white as snow. We passed on and came to the ferry, and the money that we had was just enough to pay for our ferriage."

Source:
https://www.familysearch.org/tree/person/memories/
KWCT-N65

Chapter Seventy-One

What Else Should Have Been the Outcome

One day in 1974, Brother Blaine Taylor came from work in the oil fields of Iran and received a phone call from his Muslim friend, Masoud Akhbari, informing him that Masoud's 18-month-old daughter was had been sent home from the hospital to die. She was suffering from amebic dysentery and the doctors had given up on her.

Blaine felt an overwhelming desire to give little Fiona a blessing. Masoud told him that she was in a coma and had lost half her body weight to the illness. Could Fiona receive a blessing or was that a privilege just for members of The Church of Jesus Christ of Latter-day Saints? Blaine assured him that the "Priesthood of Jesus Christ was meant for the benefit of all mankind."

Blaine collected Brother Curfew, another priesthood holder, and went to Masoud's home. A crowd of many people were gathered to conduct little Fiona across the veil of death. Upon seeing Fiona, Blaine picked her up in his arms. Brother Curfew anointed her. Blaine described what happened next:

> "I was then going to seal the anointing, when a heavenly being appeared and put his left hand on my right shoulder, and whispered into my right ear. He told me to bless this baby with health and strength and because he was a Messenger from Heaven, that I didn't need to seal the anointing and leave it in God's hands, I

should seal the priesthood blessing on her little head. I was given further instructions, which I followed explicitly."

At the close of the blessing, Blaine turned to Masoud and told them they were going back to the hospital. With the babe in his arms, Blaine walked into the hospital and he said:

"Bold as brass, I addressed myself to the receptionist, asking for the chief of staff of the hospital, and further that it should be without delay. This doctor came right out. I gave him the instructions I had previously been given about an I.V., and exactly what should be in it. He almost saluted me, but quickly turned on his heel and commanded a gurney be brought forward. All this was done in front of many hospital staff and patients, and I think it was quite a scene. I didn't care about anything except following my instructions from a Heavenly Messenger. When the gurney came, with the prescribed IV hanging on it, the doctor asked me if I should insert the needle and begin the procedure. I realized then what the impression was, and I simply said for him to do it. I spoke Farsi, the local language quite fluently, and I switched to that language. I had previously been speaking English, because that is how I was addressed in my instructions. Fiona and the family were taken to a room in the emergency ward, and we waited and prayed for her to show signs of life. In about one hour, Fiona began to move around a little, and in another hour she regained consciousness to everyone's relief, and to the utter surprise of the

hospital staff. I was not surprised. I had been given a task by a messenger from my Heavenly Father and had done what I was instructed. What else should have been the outcome?"

Blaine concludes:

"I learned from this experience that God will move you half-way around the world to touch one person's life, but that you must be willing. To be willing, you must have faith to overcome the natural fear which besets all of us. Faith and fear are incompatible!"

Source:
Story contributed by Blaine Taylor

You Saw John the Revelator

Martha Cox tells the story of a family friend who used to come stay with them while working on the St. George Temple in the 1870's. She called him, "Uncle" Allen Stout. He had been a friend and bodyguard of the Prophet Joseph Smith in Nauvoo. Martha asked him many questions, and though he was not much to volunteer information, he would answer the girl's questions. By this means, she learned much about early Church history.

One day, Martha made the statement, "I thought it could not be possible for me to see a heavenly being." Uncle Allen responded, " She might see one without recognizing it as such, as happened once with him."

Of course, that stirred Martha's curiosity, and she asked to know what had happened to him. She said:

> "He told me he was once walking with the Prophet on the west side of the Mississippi River, on the road to Montrose.... They saw a man walking along a road, leading from the south, and coming towards them. The Prophet told Allen to remain where he was while he stepped over to speak with this pedestrian. Allen turned his back towards them and for a time forgot the Prophet, and became engaged with his own thoughts, while he stood whipping a low bush with the cane he carried. The hand of the Prophet upon his shoulder aroused him.

The Prophet said, 'We must return immediately to Nauvoo.' They walked silently and rapidly. Allen became very sorrowful over his …. [lack of attention] to his duty and could not refrain from weeping. The Prophet asked him why he wept. Allen confessed, 'I am an inefficient bodyguard—criminally neglectful of your welfare. I allowed that man you met to speak with you, without being even ready to defend if he attacked you. He could have killed you and made his escape without me knowing who he is, which way he went, or what he even looks like. You will have to dispense with my services and take a guard on which you can depend. Your life is too precious to be trusted to my care.' The Prophet then said, 'That man would not harm me. You saw John the Revelator.'"

Source:
https://www.familysearch.org/tree/person/memories/MC5R-PL6

73
Chapter Seventy-Three

He Was So Nice

Generally, the pioneers walked the entire journey across
the plains and forded the rivers as they went. They
were not usually tough and seasoned frontiersmen, but
rather, city-folk not accustomed to sleeping outdoors
and life on the trail. With these things in mind, please
consider this account by Sarah Jane Allgood, who
came across the plains in 1864 as part of the Joseph
S. Rawlins wagon company. She was only 15 years old
when they departed. She wrote:

"There was a companion of mine named
Emma Ward. We came from the same place.
We walked, slept, and ate together. One day,
we walked until we were just given out. We
sat down and said we couldn't go any further.
We sat there until the wagons were just like
little specks in the distance. Our feet were so
sore and blistered; we just didn't care. While
sitting there, a young man came to us on a
horse. We didn't see where he came from nor
where he went, but he talked to us very nicely
and encouraged us to go on. He promised us
if we would try, we would make it alright, and
would not be harmed. We were so tired….out,
we didn't care whether we died or lived. But he
was so nice, and gave us such encouragement,
that it seemed to make us feel better, and have
added strength. So, we got up and went on. It
was after dark when we got to the wagon train.
We arrived at the camping place just as a hastily

organized band of men were starting back to search for us. We received a severe lecture for separating from the wagons as Indians were all around us, having passed many places where other wagon trains had been burned. The numerous newly made graves were a grim threat of what our fate would be if the Indians found us. Since then, I have told people about the man on the horse, and they have said that they think maybe it was one of the "Three Nephites"–and I truly believe it was."

Sarah and her family arrived in the Salt Lake Valley in October 1864.

Source:
https://history.churchofjesuschrist.org/overlandtravel/ sources/5338897923148855460-eng/sarah-jane-allgood-in-biographical-information-relating-to-mormon-pioneer-overland-travel-database?firstName=Sarah%20Jane&surname=Allgood

The Battle Has Begun

The mind and heart of God are not the mind and heart of men. What is worthy of remembering in the eyes of God is often trivial and of no consequence to men. In that light, this story is an effort to remember a monumental moment in the eternal affairs of this earth. It is dedicated to those modern warriors of light, anxiously engaged in the cause of Christ.

Late one fall evening after Heber and Vilate Kimball had retired to their bed, they were awakened suddenly by a sharp knocking at their door. A neighbor, John Greene, stood at the door and bade them come out and see the incredible scenery in the heavens.

They did so, and it was a beautiful starlit New England night, so exceptionally clear and brilliant that Heber said later he could have seen to pick up a pin.

As the little group watched, a white smoke or cloud formed on the eastern horizon, and slowly began to rise upward. As it did so, it formed itself into a belt spreading across the sky toward the southwest, and it was accompanied by the sound of a rushing, mighty wind.

Gradually, that belt flattened out and broadened across into a bow – like a rainbow, becoming transparent with a bluish cast, and stretching from horizon to horizon.

No sooner had that bow formed, than an army of men appeared arising from the east, and began marching twelve abreast across the bow toward the west. As vivid and real as men in the flesh, they marched in the most profound order, every man stepping in the tracks of his leader in perfect synchronization. They were dressed in the full battle gear of 19th century soldiers – muskets and bayonets. They were so clear and distinct that Heber and the small group of neighbors could distinguish the features of their faces, and hear the jingle of their equipage as they moved.

Shortly, the entire bow from horizon to horizon was crowded and filled with marching men, the sound of that marching reaching clearly to the ears of the astonished onlookers.

Heber later described the event this way:

"No man could judge of my feelings when I beheld that army of men, as plainly as ever I saw armies of men in the flesh; it seemed as though every hair of my head was alive."

When the celestial army reached the western horizon, they were met by an opposing force, and a battle ensued. The noise of the rush of men, and the clash of the arms, was distinct and unmistakable. Heber and his friends looked upon this scene for hours and till [until] finally it gradually disappeared.

Heber's wife, somewhat afraid, turned to one of the older men in the group and asked, "Father Young, what does all this mean?"

"Why, it's one of the signs of the coming of the Son of Man," he replied.

Indeed, it was, even though the world missed it, just as surely as the meridian world missed the birth of Christ. For you see, that momentous night marked the commencement of the marvelous work and wonder spoken of by Isaiah – that oh, so significant night – that night of nights eternally was September 22, 1827; the same night that just 20 miles away at a place called Cumorah, a young man named Joseph Smith was receiving the plates of The Book of Mormon from an angel named Moroni.

The war in heaven never ended. It just changed battlefields, and once more the battle between good and evil had begun. Welcome to the war!

STORYTELLER - GLENN RAWSON

ABOUT THE AUTHOR

Glenn Rawson has been telling stories for over 30 years. He started writing as a way to share his thoughts with his family and a few close friends. An acquaintance who worked in radio asked him to record and share his stories with his audience. Listeners enjoyed hearing them and the recording quickly spread to dozens of other stations throughout the country.

Glenn has authored more than 20 books and written and produced over 100 TV documentaries. Over the years, he has connected with millions of people through print, radio and TV broadcasts, and online social media channels. In 2019, he launched glennrawsonstories.com and now delivers uplifting stories to tens of thousands of people each week.

Glenn loves to research and write, but is happiest when he is traveling the world as a tour guide, sharing stories of history and the communities he visits with his guests. His goal is to help inspire and lift others with his stories.

Glenn and his wife Debbie have seven children and eighteen grandchildren.

For information about receiving weekly stories and other books available, please visit

glennrawsonstories.com or historyofthesaints.org.

Make Sure You Are Signed Up For Next Year's Stories

FREE WEEKLY STORIES DELIVERED TO YOUR INBOX

Subscribe at
GlennRawsonStories.com